SAT

VOCABULARY EXPRESS

SAT VOCABULARY EXPRESS

Word Puzzles
Designed to Decode the New SAT

Jacqueline Byrne / Michael Ashley

McGRAW-HILL

New York / Chicago / San Francisco / Lisbon / London / Madrid / Mexico City
Milan / New Delhi / San Juan / Seoul / Singapore / Sydney / Toronto

The **McGraw·Hill** *Companies*

1 2 3 4 5 6 7 8 9 10   FGR/FGR   0 9 8 7 6 5 4

ISBN 0-07-144326-6

Permission to reprint SAT materials does not constitute review or endorsement by Educational Testing Service or the College Board of this publication as a whole or of any other questions or testing information it may contain.

The words from the Hidden Meanings Puzzles and the Word within Word Creation Puzzles were taken from *The Random House Webster's Unabridged Dictionary, Second Edition,* by Random House, Inc., copyright © 1997, 1996, 1993, 1987 by Random House, Inc. Used by permission of Random House, Inc.

 This book is printed on recycled, acid-free paper containing a minimum of 50% recycled, de-inked fiber.

To Laura Brindle,
my wonderful mother-in-law,
who made it possible for me to write this book
and who also helped
create several of the puzzles.
JB

Contents

Acknowledgments

A special thank you to my students; you know who you are. You are wonderful, funny, creative, and dedicated, and I enjoy the time I spend with you. However, your lack of progress when I tried to increase your vocabulary was so frustrating that I came up with the idea for this book. Thank you!

Alexandra Sanford convinced me to tutor for the verbal SAT in addition to the writing exam when we began Ivy Educational Services. She is a fantastic teacher, and I am grateful to her for all that she has taught me.

My terrific husband, Steve Byrne, handled our four toddlers while I stole the hours to work over the last year. He could give lessons on diapering squirming triplets quickly. Thank you to the many people who kept our busy household going so I could sneak in some sleep or some work, depending on the day! In addition to my mother-in-law, Tara Baker, Maria and Roman Binek, and Elaine McManus are my guardian angels.

Michael Ashley is a great puzzler and a terrific writing partner and editor. I hope we collaborate on many more books.

Our agent, Adam Chromy of Artists and Artisans, Inc., deserves special thanks. He made our concept better and our book proposal more sophisticated. Adam sold our book quickly and handled the contract negotiations very professionally. We are lucky to have him as our agent, and you would be too.

It has been a pleasure to work with our team at McGraw-Hill. Our editor, Barbara Gilson, has championed this book from the beginning. Adrinda Kelly, Maureen B. Walker, Christopher Chew, the copywriting and design staff, and the sales people have been professional and supportive.

Bibliography

www.collegeboard.com

National Association of College Admission Counselors, *The State of College Admission 2002–2003*, 2003.

Foreword

Some of you might wonder why the world needs yet another test preparation book, and others will question just how much a student will learn from an SAT vocabulary book that focuses on solving puzzles, playing games, and having fun. The puzzles and games in *SAT Vocabulary Express* will teach students to decode the new SAT and will increase their active vocabulary and, therefore, their scores on all college admission tests.

Researchers have shown that memorizing a list of SAT vocabulary words is not an effective way to actually remember words when taking a test, and memorizing word definitions doesn't help you when you run into a word you've never seen before. The authors of this book have combined their vast knowledge of students and games into an intellectual challenge that will increase your vocabulary, teach you how to tackle new words, and teach you to associate unknown words with words you already know in order to figure out the meaning.

The most effective way to learn vocabulary is to play word games that continually challenge your mind to take words apart and put them together in a variety of ways. When you add the stimulation of having fun, your brain is more likely to retain the word skills and to more easily recall them in a test situation. The more you view test taking as a game, the more competitive and successful you will be.

Combining a test preparation expert with a nationally known crossword puzzle constructor was a stroke of genius. My students will all be given a copy of this book so that they can learn to decode the words on the SAT and other college admission tests.

You will be challenged and you will have fun; by the end of *SAT Vocabulary Express* you will have learned the art of deciphering new words. You will have developed the perseverance and confidence you need to know that you can conquer unfamiliar words, even if the new word seems overwhelming at first. The vocabulary on the new SAT will not scare you after you have finished this book because you will have learned decoding strategies that work on any word used on any of the college admission tests, even those in the most difficult questions.

The time you spend on this book will help you for years beyond the SAT. Your college professors will love that you have the ability to understand and use a powerful vocabulary. And it goes without saying that English and history majors will develop the cornerstone of their career passion—a huge repertoire of sophisticated words. Science majors will be able to quickly dissect new words and understand their meanings. Math majors will find that word problems are easier to understand and solve. And an increased vocabulary will help you to enjoy reading for the rest of your life.

Congratulations on the wise decision to use this book to prepare for the new SAT. You will be well prepared to decode the vocabulary on the SAT-I, SAT-II, and the ACT if you have completed *SAT Vocabulary Express*.

Mary Carter O'Connor
Former Director of the Rocky Mountain Office of The College Board
President, Higher Education Consultants Association

Letter to Students

Dear Students:

SAT Vocabulary Express is your password to the special mindset you will need to score well on the SAT I Reasoning Test. By using puzzle games to teach you about the SAT test-taking game, we will show you how to face off against the writers at the Educational Testing Service (the people who create the SAT) and win.

This book has been specially designed to teach you how to crack the code of the new SAT. This is not just another vocabulary book with long lists of words you are supposed to memorize before taking the test. To score well on the new SAT, it is not enough to have a good vocabulary. You have to be able to play with words—to pull them apart into their pieces, to understand their connotations, and to see the word games the test writers are playing with you.

As you do the puzzles in this book, you will learn many new words and you will become more confident in your ability to figure out the meanings of the words you don't know. Your ability to decipher increasingly sophisticated puzzles will mirror your ability to analyze difficult SAT questions. Even your performance on the math questions will be helped by the careful reading and word analysis skills you will learn in *SAT Vocabulary Express*.

The SAT is like a soccer game. When you are chasing opponents on the soccer field, do you think, "These guys are good; they'll probably beat me so I'll just let them run toward the goal?" Of course you don't. You imagine all the things you can do to your opponents to stop them. You don't quit. You are a winner.

The SAT is hard; that's what makes it interesting. In order to beat the opposing team, you study the person you will be matched against. So, in addition to studying for the SAT, study how to play the game. Develop a strategy. For example, test writers put words they know you don't know in the difficult verbal questions. Mean? No, entertaining! The writers know you don't know the definition so they leave you a clue to see if you are persistent enough to figure out the correct answer without knowing what the unknown word means. Your job is to figure out the clue, not to skip the question in defeat. In the real world these clues may not be very exciting, but in the alternate SAT universe these are moments of challenge and intrigue. Enjoy them.

This book is your password to the new SAT. As you work your way through the puzzles in this book, not only will you learn how to score well on the SAT, but you will also enjoy developing the skills you need to succeed. Word puzzles are fun, so much fun that approximately 30 million people attempt a crossword puzzle at least once a week. Word puzzles are also one of the few things you can do for fun that your parents and teachers will approve of. How often do your parents encourage you to play games when you should be studying? This book is the perfect cross between studying for the SATs and having a good time. We think we have finally found a way to make the SAT fun and challenging to study for. Impossible? Venture on.

Good luck,

Jacqueline Byrne

Michael Ashley

How to Use This Book to Crack the Code of the New SAT

SAT Vocabulary Express is a new kind of SAT vocabulary study guide that uses word puzzles to teach you many new vocabulary words and many new ways to decode words. *SAT Vocabulary Express* is organized to gradually increase both your vocabulary and your ability to determine word meanings from word roots, prefixes, and suffixes. We also teach you to master the puzzle types included in this book. The puzzles, and the vocabulary in them, will become increasingly sophisticated. The easy puzzles are equivalent to the easy questions on the SAT, the medium puzzles are equivalent to the medium SAT questions, and the challenging puzzles are equivalent to the most difficult SAT questions.

As we introduce each kind of puzzle we first explain why this kind of puzzle will help you to increase your score on the critical reading sections of the new SAT so that you will know exactly what you are learning as you make your way through this book. Then we teach you how to do the various puzzle types. Even if you think you are familiar with a particular puzzle type, it is worth reading these sections because we have included tips to help you work quickly through the puzzles. As Shakespeare said, "To climb steep hills requires slow pace at first," so all the puzzles following the introductory information are easy enough to allow you to get comfortable with the puzzle type before we start increasing the difficulty level of the words and the puzzles.

The new SAT has the following sections: sentence completions, critical reading, writing skills, math, and an essay. This book is a code breaker for the vocabulary in each section, particularly the sentence completion and critical reading sections.

A quick note for those of you who think you are wasting your time by studying for the SAT since it is a one-time test. The test-taking skills you learn now will help you in college and later, in your career. Many colleges use standardized tests for large lecture classes; many careers have required professional certifications which are attained by taking standardized tests. Learning to decode what is written will help you as you continue your education and pursue your career. And, with this book, we hope to engender a lifelong love of words, word puzzles, and reading.

SENTENCE COMPLETION QUESTIONS: You are asked to follow the logic of a sentence in order to fill in one or two blanks from a list of answer choices. In the difficult questions both the logic and the vocabulary become more sophisticated. The vocabulary in the sentence itself and in the answer choices can be problematic. This book will teach you to find clues within the unknown word and within the sentence so that you can guess most effectively on the SAT when you cannot definitively choose the correct answer.

CRITICAL READING QUESTIONS: At first glance, you may think increasing your vocabulary will not make a big difference in the critical reading section of the SAT. We disagree. The SAT test writers choose passages for you to read that will be challenging to the majority of high school juniors and seniors; one of the reasons the passages are challenging is that the authors use vocabulary that is unfamiliar to high school students. The puzzles in this book are designed to help you pull apart the word you do not know to look for roots, prefixes, or suffixes that you do recognize. If you do not find sufficient clues in the word itself, this book will also provide strategies for finding clues in the surrounding prose by teaching you to look at word connotations to give you hints as to word meaning.

WRITING SKILLS: This book will increase your vocabulary in a way that will allow you to use new words in your essay. When you memorize a long list of words, you may know what the word means, but, because you have never used the word, it is not a functional part of your vocabulary. It is unlikely that you would use a word you know the meaning of but have never used before in an essay on the SAT. When you learn new words by doing puzzles, on the other hand, you are learning new words by using them. When you finish this book, you will have pulled your new vocabulary words apart, put them together again with different beginnings or endings, and matched them with synonyms. The new words that you learn through the puzzles in this book will have become a functional, living part of your vocabulary. Your essay will benefit because you will be able to access a larger vocabulary to choose the most appropriate word to convey your thoughts.

In one of the sections of the writing skills portion of the new SAT you will be asked to identify sentence errors. These errors are frequently grammatical but can also include other types of writing errors. Several questions will include a vocabulary word that is used incorrectly or is perhaps the wrong word entirely. The word included in the sentence is always similar to the correct word, but its meaning is very different. For example, the most appropriate word for the sentence may be *exculpate*, but the test writer would insert the word *excruciate* instead. After completing *SAT Vocabulary Express,* you will be able to spot differences among words, and your increased vocabulary will help you answer these tricky questions correctly.

This book will help you to feel much more confident as you take the new SAT. Now, if you do not know the meaning of a word, you will have several strategies for deciphering the word itself. You will know how to think like the test writers so that you will be able to spot the clues they leave for students. You will answer more questions correctly because you will know more vocabulary. You will increase your score by being able to eliminate more answer choices in the questions you are unsure of, increasing the chance that you will have guessed correctly. And, because you will be in the habit of reading carefully and looking for clues, your performance on the word problems in the math section of the SAT will benefit. Let's get started.

Our delight in any particular study, art, or science rises and improves in proportion to the application which we bestow upon it. Then, what was at first an exercise becomes at length an entertainment.

Joseph Addison

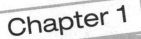

SAT DECODER: INCREASE YOUR VOCABULARY

HOW CROSSWORD PUZZLES WILL HELP YOU RAISE YOUR SAT SCORE

In an interview in Newsweek, *Norman Mailer revealed that he solves* The New York Times *crossword puzzle every day. "You have to understand," he explained, "this is how I comb my brain every morning." (Article by Will Shortz,* The New York Times *Connecticut Section, March 9, 2003.)*

Solving Crossword Puzzles Increases Your Vocabulary

In a crossword puzzle built around common SAT words, you must think of all the possible words for a definition or clue and try to come up with a word that will fit in the given blanks, rejecting the longer and shorter possibilities and homing in on the correct length answer. You will go back and forth many times between the clue and the known letters in search of that answer. For example, if the clue is "eager to fight," then you may come up with *belligerent* or *antagonistic* (one letter too many). If you have no idea what the answer is, then you can try to figure out the surrounding words. Perhaps you will fill in "B_L_." Since *bellum* means *war* in Latin, perhaps you will be able to guess that the first four letters of the clue are "BELL." Those additional letters will provide clues to more of the surrounding words, and so on. The more time you spend playing with a word in a puzzle, the more likely you are to remember the word. Increasing your SAT vocabulary will help you increase your score on every section of the SAT—including the word problems in the math section.

1

Crossword Puzzles Help You Learn to Play with Words

Puzzles are a challenge, as is the SAT. Both challenge you to persevere either through the clues or through the questions. In the more difficult SAT questions your ability to pick your way through clues mirrors your ability to pick your way through a puzzle. You can feel confident that you are ready to take the SAT when you can work through each question, whether or not you know the vocabulary. That ability comes from knowing how to figure out the connections among words and how to pull words apart into their prefixes and roots. In addition to the many puzzles in *SAT Vocabulary Express* designed just to teach word roots, crossword puzzles provide myriad opportunities for you to become comfortable building words and taking them apart. The following sentence completion question is taken from a previously released SAT[1]. It shows you how valuable the skills you will learn from crossword puzzles can be:

> Someday technology may make a door-to-door mail delivery seem _____, that is, as incongruous as a pony express delivery would seem now.
>
> (A) recursive
>
> (B) contemporaneous
>
> (C) predictable
>
> (D) anachronistic
>
> (E) revered

The SAT test writers are playing a game with you. The test writers include words they know you don't know and then leave you clues to see if you are smart enough to find them. Let's look at this question closely. SAT sentence completion questions are considered difficult if the vocabulary is unfamiliar to most students, if the sentence logic is convoluted, and if the relationship between the two blanks is sophisticated. This question is difficult because of the vocabulary, both in the question and in the answer choices. The logic of the sentence is also sophisticated, though they gave you a break by including only one blank. At first glance, the vocabulary in this question will make you want to throw up your hands in defeat and move on to the next question. Not so fast.

In the question itself, the word *incongruous* is probably not familiar, and without a general meaning of incongruous it will be impossible to answer the question correctly. Does incongruous sound like any other word you know? How about congruent from math class? Congruent triangles are identical triangles. Therefore, incongruous must mean "not the same as" or "not compatible." Now we are getting somewhere. According to the logic of the sentence, a pony express

---

[1]SAT test materials selected from 10 Real SATs, 2000. Reprinted by permission of the College Entrance Examination Board, the copyright owner.

delivery does not fit in today's world. The sentence is suggesting that someday door-to-door mail delivery will not seem to fit into the world. So, we are looking for a word that will suggest "out of place" or incompatible, or incongruous.

If we move on to the answer choices, we can see that the test writers are still playing games with us. Choice C is easy to eliminate; A can go out also because the prefix *re* meaning "repeat or redo" has nothing to do with the word we are searching for. That still leaves three choices. Choice B, contemporaneous, should look like a word you do know, contemporary, meaning current, of the present time. That eliminates B because it is the opposite of what we are looking for. Choice D is frightening until you pick it into pieces. Does *chron* look familiar? It should. Think of all of the words you know with chron in them—chronological, chronic, chronograph. *Chron* means time. Immediately your SAT correct answer antennae should go up. Choice E is not a game unfortunately, but it is a joke. The test writers actually expect you to know the Latin root for respect, vereri, not a game at all. But the test writers chose *revered* because Paul Revere rode a horse to give a message to people, just as the pony express did. See, the test writers are human after all. And funny, sort of.

Where does that leave us with this difficult sentence completion question? Let's say that we were able to eliminate everything except choices D and E. Your best bet would be to go with choice D since you know that the concept of time is included in that word choice. In fact, D is the correct answer. Anachronistic means existing or happening at other than its proper or historical time (*ana* = backward and *khronizein* = to belong in time in Greek).

While it took us many words to write out the correct approach toward a sentence completion question with unknown vocabulary, you should be able to find the clues and either keep or eliminate the answer choice very quickly after doing the puzzles in this book. The clues in the sentence completion questions will help you know what kind of word (negative or positive, for example) to put in the blanks, just as the clues in a crossword puzzle help you to think of appropriate words to fill in the blank squares. Puzzles force you to think in the same way that the SAT does. There is no better way to study for a test that requires you to play with words than word puzzles since they require the same skill.

By the way, the best way to answer sentence completion questions is to plug your own word into the blank in the sentence, and then look for synonyms in the answer choices. Most students read the sentence five times, plugging each answer selection into the blanks. It is a time-consuming method that frequently ends in frustration as each answer begins to sound reasonable.

Crossword Puzzles Change Your Attitude toward the SAT

Crossword puzzles challenge you to persevere through the clues or through the questions. In the more difficult verbal SAT questions your ability to pick your way through clues mirrors your ability to pick your way through a puzzle. The pride and satisfaction you feel when you figure out a difficult puzzle will mirror your pride when you figure out a difficult SAT question.

SAT Vocabulary Express is designed to encourage you to learn to play with and remember words through puzzles. When you were younger, you learned new things through playing games and puzzles. There is no reason to stop. The SAT is a game you can win, just as you will win each time you complete one of the puzzles in *SAT Vocabulary Express*. Winners don't cower at the thought of the SAT; winners stand tall, put on their game face, and kick some butt!

CROSSWORD PUZZLE INSTRUCTIONS

GOAL: To fill in all the blank spaces in the puzzle. Crosswords are undoubtedly the most popular puzzle ever invented. It is estimated that as many as 30 million Americans attempt to solve at least one of them a week. Why such popularity? Probably because they are both simple in concept and pleasing to the eye. When finished, you get complete words (or the occasional abbreviation, prefix, suffix, or the like) running both across and down the diagram, seemingly part of each other yet unrelated. That's considered "elegant" to puzzle enthusiasts, meaning simple and very satisfying. Answer each of the clues beginning at the square of the clue's number, one letter per square. Answers are to be entered either across or down as the clues indicate.

WHY: Crossword puzzles are an excellent way to increase your vocabulary. Going from the definition to the word, rather than the other way around, forces you to think of synonyms. Also, you will spend time trying to figure out each word. The more time you spend with a word, the better the chance that you will remember it.

RULES: Each letter must fit with both the horizontal and the vertical word.

HINT: If you get stuck, move on to another corner or section. Eventually, everything ties together in a crossword puzzle.

Some people are just naturally likable. We enjoy their company; we enjoy being around them. And there are lots of words to describe people like this. For instance, you might call genial people "Easy going."

Crossword Puzzle 1
Easy Going

ACROSS

1. Grow old
4. President Lincoln
7. Bug that makes you sick in winter
10. Actor Gibson of "Signs"
11. Attorney's field of study
12. Michael Stipe's band
13. Sociable; easy to get along with
15. State west of Montana (abbr.)
16. Lousy although not failing grade
17. "That's one for _____"
18. Many popular video arcade games
21. Singles
24. Be appropriate for; suit
25. Home, at least to a beaver
26. Where you might order and drink a latte
27. Host Daly of TV's "Last Call"
28. "Give me _____ A!"
29. Shade of color; tint
30. Where a scientist works
32. Warm; courteous and gracious
36. Feel sick
37. Put to work or employ
38. Sound a pigeon makes
39. Dr. _____ of rap music
40. Founding Father Franklin
41. Elevated railroads, for short

DOWN

1. "I _____ good boy" (2 wds.)
2. Diamond or ruby, e.g.
3. Inventor Whitney
4. Even if
5. Bundles of cotton
6. Female sheep
7. David Schwimmer's sitcom
8. Had the pack at one's heels
9. Actress Thurman of "Kill Bill"
14. Oscar winner Brody of "The Pianist"
17. Secured a boat with cables
18. George Lopez and Jim Belushi's network
19. Alternative to coffee
20. Easy to approach and talk to
22. What someone bragging displays
23. Member of Congress (abbr.)
25. Polo fashion designer Ralph
27. Selected
30. Young boy
31. What we breathe
32. Baby bear
33. Diamonds, to a burglar
34. MSN and Yahoo rival
35. _____ Angeles, California

Some people love words—lots of words. And they use lots of words, all the time. We sometimes say that these people are too wordy. Or that they are "All talk."

Crossword Puzzle 2
All Talk

ACROSS

1. Sing with closed lips
4. Unhappy
7. This goes on your head
10. _____ rule (generally) (2 wds.)
11. TV rival of SHO or MAX
12. Plural form of "is"
13. Wordy; possibly too wordy
15. Actress Thompson of "Back to the Future"
16. Follow in order or afterward
17. Headliner in a movie
18. Maker of Orange Crush soda
19. Best bud
21. Inclined to chat a lot
25. Put on, like The Eagles' Henley
26. Offer, as a present
28. A rolling stone won't gather this
31. Cut into small pieces
32. Genetic messenger material, for short
33. Chattering excessively; babbling
35. Will Ferrell Christmas movie and role of 2003
36. Stimpy's bud
37. General Grant's opposite at Appomattox
38. Hair coloring material
39. Not even
40. Actors Harris and Asner

DOWN

1. Place of safety or refuge
2. Branch of the Web linking newsgroups
3. Actress Thomason of "The Haunted Mansion" (anagram of "ashram")
4. This goes on your foot
5. Workout target after the pecs, maybe
6. Female deer
7. "Stop right there!"
8. Length times width product
9. Rip up
14. Constructs a house
17. Small in amount or degree
19. Stove-top cooking utensil or bad movie review
20. _____ that time (then)
22. Boxing match win, for short
23. Masculine or manly
24. Balanced out two piles equally
27. Cutting parts of knives
28. Talking horse of TV sitcom fame (2 wds.)
29. Without anything further
30. Umpire's call at a base
31. You'll find plenty of this at the beach
33. Not an amateur
34. One of the three primary colors

We use a lot of different words to express negative things or situations. Sometimes we use a lot of negative words when we're trying to explain ourselves. And sometimes we get confused. Are you worried we'll confuse you? Well, don't, because this is "not" a puzzle. In fact, we'll "Puzzle you—Not!"

Crossword Puzzle 3
Puzzle You—Not!

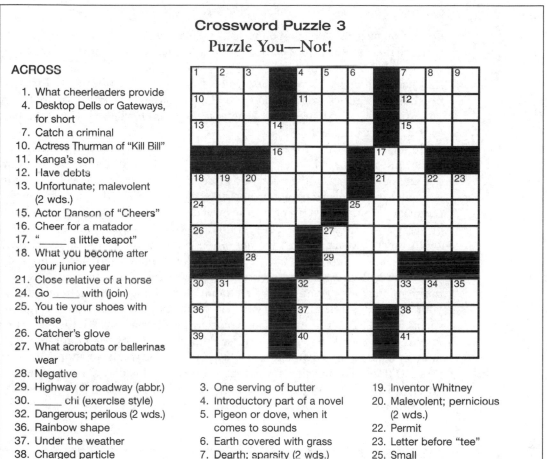

ACROSS

1. What cheerleaders provide
4. Desktop Dells or Gateways, for short
7. Catch a criminal
10. Actress Thurman of "Kill Bill"
11. Kanga's son
12. I have debts
13. Unfortunate; malevolent (2 wds.)
15. Actor Danson of "Cheers"
16. Cheer for a matador
17. "_____ a little teapot"
18. What you become after your junior year
21. Close relative of a horse
24. Go _____ with (join)
25. You tie your shoes with these
26. Catcher's glove
27. What acrobats or ballerinas wear
28. Negative
29. Highway or roadway (abbr.)
30. _____ chi (exercise style)
32. Dangerous; perilous (2 wds.)
36. Rainbow shape
37. Under the weather
38. Charged particle
39. Hive resident
40. Ginger _____ (soda)
41. Had everyone behind you in the race

DOWN

1. Play on words
2. Weezer or Jawbreaker's music
3. One serving of butter
4. Introductory part of a novel
5. Pigeon or dove, when it comes to sounds
6. Earth covered with grass
7. Dearth; sparsity (2 wds.)
8. Bowl over, overwhelm with fear
9. Place where you sleep
14. Enter a room (2 wds.)
17. Physical likenesses; photographs
18. "I Am _____" (Sean Penn movie)
19. Inventor Whitney
20. Malevolent; pernicious (2 wds.)
22. Permit
23. Letter before "tee"
25. Small
27. Mythical giant cave dweller
30. PC button that sets indents
31. "We _____ the Champions!"
32. Actress Vardalos of "My Big Fat Greek Wedding"
33. Be under the weather
34. Enemy
35. Conclusion

HOW QUOTATION PUZZLES WILL HELP YOU RAISE YOUR SAT SCORE

The acrostic (quotation puzzle) was probably invented about the same time with the anagram, tho' it is impossible to decide whether the inventor of the one or the other were the greater blockhead. Joseph Addison

Quotation puzzles will help you to increase your verbal SAT score in the same ways that crossword puzzles do. Quotation puzzles are another interesting way to learn new words.

Quotation puzzles will prepare you for the SAT in another way. There are two basic categories from which the SAT "persuasive" essay topics are taken: quotation essay and issue essay. The quotation puzzle will help you to prepare for the quotation essay.

In a quotation puzzle you are asked to figure out words based on their definition, just as you are in a crossword puzzle. Each letter of the word you figure out will have a place in the quotation grid. When the quotation grid is filled in, you will have revealed a quotation and its author. If you spend a moment figuring out what the author was trying to convey and whether or not you agree with him or her, you will be preparing yourself for an SAT essay based upon a quotation.

In order to score well on the quotation essay on the SAT, you must determine what the author meant and how you feel about what the author said. Then you will create a simple outline to ensure that you are supporting your position in favor of or opposing the author's viewpoint. With the remainder of your 25-minute time allotment you will write your essay. The 3 or 4 minutes spent figuring out the quotation, your position, and your outline are very important and will enable you to raise your score. Test graders are interested in how logical your argument is and whether or not you have supported your thesis with at least three examples from literature, history, current events, or your own life. If you spend time thinking about the quotation before you start to write, you will be able to write a more cohesive essay.

QUOTATION PUZZLE INSTRUCTIONS

GOAL: Not surprisingly, quotation puzzles ask you to discover a quotation and then its author.

WHY: Quotation puzzles are another interesting way to learn new words. The quotation makes it more fun. You won't believe what some people say.

RULES: Answer as many of the clues below the diagram as you can, one letter per numbered blank. Then transfer each letter to the appropriately numbered square in the diagram. You will see the words and phrases of a quotation begin emerging, reading from left to right, with the black squares indicating the spaces between words. Working back and forth from the diagram to the numbered blanks, you can finish the puzzle. As a bonus, the author of the quote is at its end. Although these may appear impossibly difficult at first, quotation puzzles actually get easier to solve as you go along.

HINT: Look for prepositional phrases such as "in the," "on the," "out of," and so on in the quote. Also, remember that "the" is the most common three-letter word in English.

Quotation Puzzle 1

1C	2H	■	3E	4H	5A	■	6D	7F	8B	9E	■	10A	11B	12H	13G	■	14A
15C	16E	17H	■	18A	19D	20C	21B	22E	23G	24F	■	25B	26D	■	27A	28D	29B
30C	■	31C	32H	33A	34E	■	35A	36F	37G	38H	39B	40D	■	41F	42G	43D	44A
45C	46B	■	47D	48G	49B	50F	51E	52C	■								

Clues:

A. Baseball's Sultan of Swat (2 wds.)

___ ___ ___ ___ ___ ___ ___ ___
10 18 35 33 44 5   14 27

B. Regard or treat with reverence

___ ___ ___ ___ ___ ___ ___ ___
29 39 8   46 49 21 25 11

C. Naomi Watts movie about a sinister videotape (2 wds.)

___ ___ ___ ___ ___ ___ ___
31 15 30 20 1   52 45

D. "Masked" American mammal

___ ___ ___ ___ ___ ___ ___
19 28 47 6   43 26 40

E. Hostility; hatred; ill will

___ ___ ___ ___ ___ ___
16 22 34 51 9   3

F. Bird symbol of the United States

___ ___ ___ ___ ___
36 7   41 50 24

G. Playing marble with curved, colored bands

___ ___ ___ ___ ___
48 23 37 13 42

H. Get to the bottom of or to understand

___ ___ ___ ___ ___ ___
2   12 38 32 4   17

Quotation Puzzle 2

1F	2D		3G	4E	5B		6G	7C	8F	9A	10I		11B	12E		13J	14I
15E	16F		17J	18A		19F	20A	21I	22G	23B	24D	25C	26H		27G	28H	29I
30J		31D	32G		33C	34B	35E	36J	37D	38I		39F	40C	41B	42A	43J	44H
	45A	46C	47H	48B	49E		50B	51D	52J	53H	54E		55C	56F	57E	58A	

Clues:

A. Plato and Socrates's home town

     20   42   58   45   9   18

B. State of great commotion or confusion

     41   5   23   11   50   34   48

C. Rock music's brother trio of "Runaway Run"

     7   46   55   33   40   25

D. Eskimo ice home

     24   51   37   31   2

E. Word having nearly the same meaning as another

     57   12   15   4   54   49   35

F. Capital city of Spain

     19   56   1   39   8   16

G. "_____, Madly, Deeply" (Savage Garden hit song)

     6   32   22   27   3

H. Test score mark

     26   47   28   44   53

I. Pet name for a cat

     10   14   29   21   38

J. Retard progress with obstructions or obstacles

     17   13   36   30   52   43

HOW ANAGRAM MAGIC SQUARE PUZZLES WILL HELP YOU RAISE YOUR SAT SCORE

Anagram magic square puzzles are fun, and they should be a little easier than some of our other puzzles. They will help you to prepare for the SAT in the same way that crossword puzzles will.

ANAGRAM MAGIC SQUARE PUZZLE INSTRUCTIONS

GOAL: To figure out the long SAT word at the bottom of the page.

WHY: Many people enjoy solving anagrams, so much so that doing so has for many years been a game in itself. You'll have to mentally scramble letters to form words. Here, each five-letter word on our list can be rearranged to form an entirely new five-letter word. But there's a twist: as in a challenging quotation puzzle, the first letters of these new words will, when put in order, spell out a new, nine-letter word. Enter those first letters in the numbered blanks at the bottom of the page.

RULES: In each square below is a five-letter word. Below the squares is a list of numbered clues. Find which clue belongs with the words in the squares and write the number of the clue in the small space inside the large square. Write an anagram of each word on the dotted line. The first letter of each answer is to be entered on the corresponding numbered blank below the squares, giving the SAT vocabulary word whose definition is in parentheses.

HINT: Having trouble with an anagram? Try working backwards from the final answer: Can you make out a prefix or a suffix there, even if you haven't figured out the entire SAT word?

Anagram Magic Square Puzzle 1

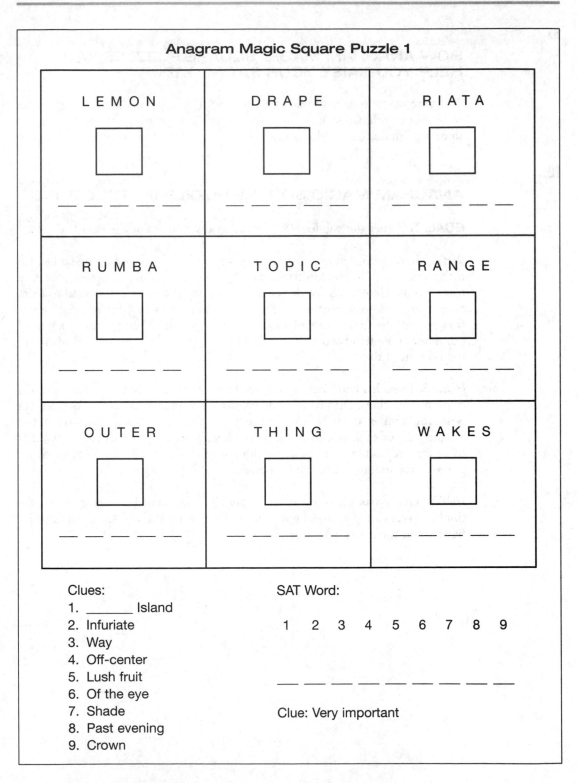

L E M O N	D R A P E	R I A T A
☐	☐	☐
_ _ _ _ _	_ _ _ _ _	_ _ _ _ _
R U M B A	T O P I C	R A N G E
☐	☐	☐
_ _ _ _ _	_ _ _ _ _	_ _ _ _ _
O U T E R	T H I N G	W A K E S
☐	☐	☐
_ _ _ _ _	_ _ _ _ _	_ _ _ _ _

Clues:
1. _____ Island
2. Infuriate
3. Way
4. Off-center
5. Lush fruit
6. Of the eye
7. Shade
8. Past evening
9. Crown

SAT Word:

1   2   3   4   5   6   7   8   9

_ _ _ _ _ _ _ _ _

Clue: Very important

Anagram Magic Square Puzzle 2

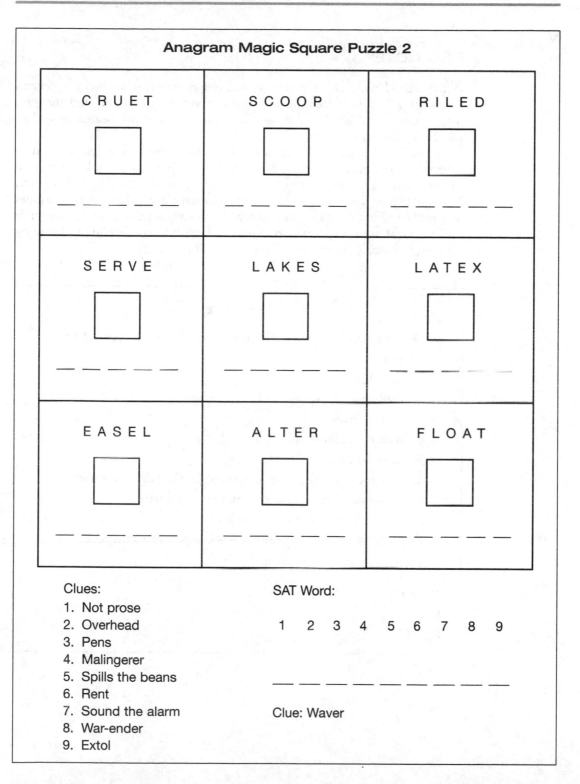

CRUET

SCOOP

RILED

— — — — —

— — — — —

— — — — —

SERVE

LAKES

LATEX

— — — — —

— — — — —

— — — — —

EASEL

ALTER

FLOAT

— — — — —

— — — — —

— — — — —

Clues:
1. Not prose
2. Overhead
3. Pens
4. Malingerer
5. Spills the beans
6. Rent
7. Sound the alarm
8. War-ender
9. Extol

SAT Word:

1   2   3   4   5   6   7   8   9

— — — — — — — — —

Clue: Waver

END NOTE

Nice work! You have learned new vocabulary words while you have begun the exciting process of learning how to do crossword, quotation, and anagram magic square puzzles. We hope you are intrigued and are beginning to like puzzles as much as we do.

Most importantly, you have begun to think in the special way needed to raise your score on all aspects of the new SAT. When you did not know a word in the preceding puzzles, the process of figuring out the word was important. You will master the technique of figuring out what a word means by the clues around it and within it as you make your way through this book. You have made a great start. Now we are going to learn to decode Hidden Meaning Puzzles, Cryptofamily Puzzles, and Groupie Puzzles.

Fun Quiz

1. Which section of the old SAT is not included in the new SAT?
   a. essay
   b. analogies
   c. reading comprehension
   d. critical reading
   e. sentence completion

2. What is the ACT?
   a. a financial aid program sponsored by the U.S. government
   b. the name of the drama department at Juilliard
   c. a grass-roots volunteer organization
   d. a college admission test that is a competitor to the SAT
   e. A Cool Teacher award program

Answers

1. b
2. d

Chapter 2

THE SAT DECODER: LEARN TO PLAY WITH WORDS

HOW HIDDEN MEANINGS PUZZLES WILL HELP YOU RAISE YOUR SAT SCORE

Hidden meanings puzzles will help you to score well on all aspects of the SAT that require critical reasoning skills because they create a world that is backwards; you must create a definition for a word by selecting appropriate words from a word list. Trying to *create* a definition rather than trying to guess a word from the definition as you do in crossword puzzles forces you to think differently about words. Your ability to play with words—moving from definition to word and back again—will increase your reading comprehension.

Increased reading comprehension is important if you want to do well on the critical reading portion of the SAT. Sentence completion questions ask you to read a sentence accurately so that you can insert one or two words in the blanks. There are vocabulary words in the question and in the answer choices. The sentence itself provides clues to the meanings of the words in the sentence and in the answer choices. Your ability to piece together the definition of a word you don't know will increase your ability to answer difficult sentence completion questions correctly.

Your ability to read accurately is also being tested in the reading comprehension section of the SAT. One or two passages are followed by a series of questions that test your ability to synthesize the information in the passage, to read between the lines, to decode metaphors and other sophisticated writing techniques, and to determine the meaning of a word within the context of the passage. Hidden meaning puzzles help you with all four skills:

1. In order to answer questions that ask you to determine which answer best reflects the main idea of the passage, the test writers expect that you will have understood the general tone of the passage in addition to the basic

idea. Hidden meaning puzzles help you learn to decode words so that you understand the entire passage rather than missing important parts.

2. In order to read between the lines, you must understand the words used by the author to convey his or her message. Words frequently have several definitions, the literal meaning and many connotations, the implied meanings. Your ability to determine word meaning from context is helped by doing hidden meaning puzzles which ask you to create a definition out of a list of words.

3. In order to accurately decode sophisticated writing techniques like metaphors and allusions, you must understand what the author is trying to convey. You must determine a general definition for the unknown word and figure out what the word's main connotation is. Determining whether a word is positive or negative, angry or pleased, apathetic or enthusiastic, greatly enhances your ability to read well. Hidden meaning puzzles ask you to assess the word you are trying to define and to assess the words in the word list to match defining words with the word whose definition you seek. The definition you build must reflect the connotation of the word you are trying to define.

4. In each reading comprehension section there will be one or two questions that ask you to determine the meaning of a word in the context of a particular sentence. The word you are asked to define is always used in an uncommon way. Therefore, using the context of the sentence, you must create a definition in your head the same way you do in a hidden meaning puzzle. In addition to the "word in context" questions, there are frequently other reading comprehension questions that ask you to examine a phrase or sentence to decide why the author used the phrase or sentence in the passage. Again, you are being asked to figure out the connotations elicited by the phrase or question.

HIDDEN MEANINGS PUZZLE INSTRUCTIONS

GOAL: To fill in the blanks below by referring to the word list. The numbers in parenthesis indicate how many letters the correct answer has.

WHY: Not only will you learn the words you are defining, but you will learn many synonyms as well.

RULES: Each word in the word list can be used only once; each word is used once.

HINT: Sometimes there are only one or two words listed under a word-number category, for example, 13 Letters. It should be relatively easy to figure out what word goes where when there are only one or two words in the group. If you start with easy groupings, you will get a good start on the puzzle. Also, start with words you are familiar with before trying to figure out the definitions of the words you do not know.

Hidden Meanings Puzzle 1

sub·tle (sut´l), *adj.,* **-tler, -tlest**

1. thin, _____(7), or rarefied, as a fluid or an odor.
2. fine or _____(8) in meaning or intent; _____(9) to perceive or understand.
3. delicate or faint and _____(10).

vi·a·ble (vī´ə bəl), *adj.*

1. capable of _____(6).

ac·cent (*n.* ak´sent; *v.* ak´sent, ak sent´), *n.*

1. _____(10) of a syllable in terms of differential loudness, or of _____(5), or _____(6), or of a combination of these.

fruit·less (frōōt´lis), *adj.*

1. _____(7); unproductive; without _____(7) or success.
2. bearing no fruit; _____(6).

re·serve (ri zûrv´), *v.,* **-served, -serv·ing,** *n., adj.* —*v.t.*

1. to keep back or _____(4) for future use, _____(8), treatment and so on.

draw·back (drô´bak´), *n.*

1. a _____(9) or disadvantage; an undesirable or _____(13) feature.

ho·mo·ge·ne·ous (hō´mə jē´nē əs, -jēn´yəs, hom´ə-), *adj.*

1. composed of parts or _____(8) that are all of the same kind; not _____(13).
2. of the same kind or _____(6); essentially _____(5).

re·cep·tive (ri sep´tiv), *adj.*

1. having the quality of _____(9), taking in, or _____(9).
2. able or quick to receive knowledge, _____(5), and so on.

gen·re (zhän´rə; *Fr.* zhäN´Rə), *n., pl.* **-res** (-rəz; *Fr.* -Rə), *adj.* —*n.*

1. a class or _____(8) of _____(8) endeavor having a particular form, content, technique, or the like.

res·pite (res´pit), *n., v.,* **-pit·ed, -pit·ing,** —*n.*

1. a delay or _____(9) for a time, especially of anything _____(11) or trying; an _____(8) of relief.

Hidden Meanings Puzzle 1 (continued)

4 LETTERS
SAVE

5 LETTERS
ALIKE
PITCH
IDEAS

6 LETTERS
NATURE
LIVING
BARREN
LENGTH

7 LETTERS
RESULTS
USELESS
TENUOUS

8 LETTERS
ARTISTIC
INTERVAL
ELEMENTS
CATEGORY
DELICATE
DISPOSAL

9 LETTERS
RECEIVING
CESSATION
DIFFICULT
HINDRANCE
ADMITTING

10 LETTERS
PROMINENCE
MYSTERIOUS

11 LETTERS
DISTRESSING

13 LETTERS
HETEROGENEOUS
OBJECTIONABLE

Some words in a particular definition will be interchangeable.

Hidden Meanings Puzzle 2

sur·pass (sər pas´, -päs´), *v.t.*

1. to go _____(6) in amount, extent, or degree; to be greater than; _____(6).
2. to go beyond in excellence or achievement; be superior to; _____(5).

dic·tion (dik´shən), *n.*

1. _____(5) of speaking or writing as dependent upon _____(6) of words.
2. the accent, inflection, _____(10), and speech-sound quality manifested by an individual speaker, usually judged in terms of prevailing standards of acceptability.

gen·u·ine (jen´yo͞o in), *adj.*

1. possessing the claimed or _____(10) character, quality, or origin; not _____(11); _____(9).

ten·ta·tive (ten´tə tiv), *adj.*

1. of the nature of or made or done as a trial, _____(10), or attempt.
2. unsure; _____(9); not definite or positive; _____(8).

doc·ile (dos´əl; *Brit.* do͝o´sīl), *adj.*

1. _____(6) managed or handled; _____(9).
2. readily _____(7) or taught; teachable.

com·ply (kəm plī´), *v.i.,* **-plied, -ply·ing**

1. to act or be in _____(10) with wishes, _____(8), demands, requirements, conditions, and so on; _____(5) (sometimes followed by *with*).

re·vert (ri vûrt´), *v.i.*

1. to _____(6) to a former habit, practice, _____(6), condition, and so on.
2. *Law:* to go back to or return to the former owner or to his or her _____(5).
3. *Biology:* to return to an earlier or _____(9) type.

as·sent (ə sent´), *v.i.*

1. to agree or _____(6); subscribe to (often followed by *to*).
2. to give in; _____(7); _____(5).

de·void (di void´), *adj.*

1. not _____(10), untouched by, _____(4), or destitute (usually followed by *of*).
2. to deplete or _____(5) of some quality or _____(9).

Hidden Meanings Puzzle 2 *(continued)*

se·clude (si klōōd′), *v.t.,* **-clud·ed, -clud·ing**

1. to place in or _____(8) into _____(8); remove from social contact and activity.

2. to _____(7); shut off; keep _____(5).

4 LETTERS
VOID

5 LETTERS
STRIP
AGREE
YIELD
STYLE
APART
EXCEL
HEIRS

6 LETTERS
EASILY
CONCUR
EXCEED
RETURN
BELIEF
BEYOND
CHOICE

7 LETTERS
TRAINED
ISOLATE
CONCEDE

8 LETTERS
WITHDRAW
HESITANT
REQUESTS
SOLITUDE

9 LETTERS
AUTHENTIC
SUBSTANCE
PRIMITIVE
UNCERTAIN
TRACTABLE

10 LETTERS
ACCORDANCE
POSSESSING
ATTRIBUTED
INTONATION
EXPERIMENT

11 LETTERS
COUNTERFEIT

Some words in a particular definition will be interchangeable.

HOW CRYPTOFAMILY PUZZLES WILL INCREASE YOUR SAT SCORE

Cryptofamily puzzles will increase your vocabulary, provide a link among all the words in the puzzle, and help you to guess effectively on the SAT. And they are fun.

Solving Cryptofamily Puzzles Increases Your Vocabulary

With the cryptofamily puzzles, we are asking you to decipher a single-letter substitution code to discover a list of related words. When confronted with a list of 15 related words to decode, you will first think of all of the synonyms you can that fit the title of the cryptofamily. For example, if the title word is *friendly* you will think of as many synonyms as you can for *friendly* to try to break the code on at least one word. This is a basic vocabulary building exercise until you can't come up with any more synonyms. Then, as you break the code for each word you will learn new words that also mean *friendly*. Learning new words will help you to answer more sentence completion questions correctly, read the reading comprehension section more accurately, and use the most effective word when writing your essay.

Cryptofamily Puzzles Create an Association among All the Words in the Family

In a cryptofamily with 15 words that all mean *friendly*, you may not know the nuances among the words, but you will remember that the word has a positive connotation. That knowledge in itself is frequently enough to eliminate or keep an answer choice on a difficult SAT question. If you can eliminate three answer choices for a given question, then you should guess. In the reading comprehension section, knowing approximately what a word means will help you to better understand the reading selection.

Cryptofamily Puzzles Help You to Guess Effectively on the SAT

There is a trick to use on the verbal SAT as a last resort. Your knowledge of word associations gained from doing puzzles like the cryptofamilies will ensure that you accurately determine whether a word is positive or negative. The following sentence completion question taken from a previously released SAT[1] is a good example:

> Astronomers who suspected that the sunspot cycle is not eleven years long have been _____ by studies _____ their belief that the entire cycle is actually twice that long.
>
> (A) vindicated . . . confirming
>
> (B) exonerated . . . refuting

---

[1]SAT test materials selected from 10 Real SATs, 2000. Reprinted by permission of the College Entrance Examination Board, the copyright owner.

(C) discredited . . . substantiating

(D) encouraged . . . rejecting

(E) humiliated . . . proving

If you are completely stuck on the vocabulary and about to skip the question, try to figure out whether the words are positive or negative. The resulting chart would look like this:

+ . . . +	
(A)	+ . . . +
(B)	+ . . . −
(C)	− . . . +
(D)	+ . . . −
(E)	− . . . +

Because the relationship between the words in the sentence completion is positive to positive, the only possible answer will be positive to positive or negative to negative. In this question, A is the only possible answer. On many questions this method of last resort will eliminate three answer choices. You then have a 50-50 chance of getting the correct answer without knowing what some of the words mean. Those are pretty good odds.

SAT Vocabulary Express is designed to prepare you to play the SAT game. It is unlikely that you will remember all the words you study for the SAT, so creating an association in your mind among groups of words gives you a solid place from which to guess. Especially on the difficult verbal questions, guessing intelligently is the way to a better SAT score.

CRYPTOFAMILY PUZZLE INSTRUCTIONS

GOAL: Cryptofamily puzzles ask you to play detective and break a simple, single-letter substitution code. For example, the words "good fun" might appear in the cryptofamily as "XEEL MDR." When letter X represents G, it will always be G in that family. The words in the following families are related to one another in some fashion. It's up to you to figure out how; think about synonyms. The first word is solved in each cryptofamily to give you a head start.

WHY: By solving the code in this puzzle, you will be creating an association in your mind among all these words. On the SAT, even if you don't remember the nuances among the word meanings, you will know whether the word is positive or negative and approximately what the word means.

HINT: Be aware that *e* is the most common letter in the English language. Also, the *th* combination is very common: *the, they, those, that, with, both,* and so on.
    Warning: The code is different for every new family.

Cryptofamily Puzzle 1
You Lazy Bum

V O U T O C O X I X U O V
L A C K A D A I S I C A L

O N O E B A

V O I I X E J C Z

V O Y H J G L

V Z E B O L H X U

I G N G L X K X U

E G L N G L

U G W O E G I Z

I E J N G L

N O I I X F Z

V X I E V Z I I

N B V Z H W O E X U

I G W Y G V Z Y E

V O Y H J X C

I V J H H X I B

Cryptofamily Puzzle 2
Whatever YOU Say

H U M M J C Y
P A S S I V E

L U O O Y U N O Y

U L N J C U O Y R E

C U P J O O U E Y

K N Y V J Y R E

U N Y A U R P Y

U L Y R U N O Y

N J V V U N O Y

P K L H O J U R E

E G U P E U N O Y

V Y Q Y G Y R E J U O

K N M Y S X J K X M

M Y G C J O Y

U P S X J Y M P Y R E

G Y M J B R Y V

Cryptofamily Puzzle 3 Nit-Picking	Cryptofamily Puzzle 4 I Will NEVER Give Up
D C X Y E O X *P R E C I S E*	H R D Z V P *M U L I S H*
X A G U V O I E Q X	M A V S Z T N S F
N X I E Y V H F V O	S F T N W Z M R V
O Y C V D V H F V O	C M L L F C
D C U J N U I E Y	Z T S Y N W S N A D F
I G F C F V J G K X O O	Z T S Y N T V Z L F T S
D U E K O I U B E K J	U F Y O F Y V F
F Z O X C Q U K I	I Z D D J R D
Y F N D V H O E Q X	M A V S Y F U F Y M R V
S E H E J X K I	A R D D P F N C F C
U O O E S V F V O	M A C R Y N S F
F Z O X O O E Q X	U R L T N W Z M R V
U I I X K I E Q X	C M L H N S Z W
O X S V H F V O	Z T W M Y Y Z L Z A D F
Y U C X L V H	U Z L P F N C F C

HOW GROUPIE PUZZLES WILL HELP YOU RAISE YOUR SAT SCORE

Groupies are small puzzles that will help you think of the connections among words. You will have to think of both the definition and the connotation of the listed words as you figure out the scrambled clues. The list of scrambled clues will lead you to the phrase at the bottom of the list. The reverse is also true: The unscrambled phrase will help you figure out the list of related words.

As we discuss above, connotations are important when you are figuring out difficult SAT questions. While the connotations of a word may not get you the correct answer, they can help you to narrow down the answer choices, thereby increasing the likelihood that you will deduce the correct answer.

GROUPIE PUZZLE INSTRUCTIONS

GOAL: Groupies are a blend. Like anagrams, groupies ask you to unscramble seemingly random letters to form complete words. Since the words here are much longer than our previous five-letter anagrams, we've placed a couple of letters in each word to help get you started. Next, as in hidden meanings or in a quotation puzzle, we're asking you to unscramble an even longer, but related, phrase at the bottom of the page. Tough? You bet. But with a little patience and some detective work back and forth, we're betting you can do it.

WHY: If you can figure out the connections among the words, you will be able to eliminate wrong answers and choose correct answers more easily on the SAT.

RULES: Figure out what each word is by unscrambling the letters. In each clue two letters have been placed correctly to give you a head start. Once you have all the clues unscrambled, you can try to figure out what phrase is suggested by all the clues. The letters of the words in the phrase are also scrambled, so it is possible to figure out the phrase without figuring out the connection among the words.

HINT: Once you have unscrambled some of the clue words, see if the phrase has any small words. By filling in the small words and eliminating those letters from the scrambled phrase letters, it is often possible to begin to figure out the phrase which will, in turn, help you figure out the rest of the clue words.

Groupie Puzzle 1	**Groupie Puzzle 2**

Groupie Puzzle 1

E T M R E P E D I T A

_ _ E _ _ D _ _ _ _ _

F E D J T I I S U

_ _ S T _ _ _ _ _

V E E E G N R

R _ _ _ _ _ E

L I B I L B A C

_ I _ _ I _ _ _

C I T P O L A

_ _ T _ _ _ L

A I T E L E T R A

R _ _ A _ _ _ _ _

Groupie Phrase

Y E A F Y E N R O E E

_ _ _ _ O _ _ _ E _ _

Groupie Puzzle 2

S L A G S Y

_ L _ _ S _

E N R E E S

_ E _ _ _ E

Z T O R O I N A L H

H _ _ _ _ _ N _ _ _

D O L E A S M I W T I N N O

_ _ O - _ _ _ _ _ _ _ _ _ _ L

T K E R A A F B S

_ R _ _ _ _ _ S _

F K Y O E F

_ _ F - _ E _

Groupie Phrase

P A A A A A S L K N E F C T

_ L _ _ _ _ A _ _ _ _ _ _ _

END NOTE

Good job! You are learning to play with words. Through hidden meaning puzzles you have begun to try to figure out the meaning of a word by looking at the word itself. Through cryptofamily puzzles you have started to make connections among groups of words with similar meanings. Groupies made you work a little harder to make a connection among all the words in a group. Trying to figure out the meanings and the connotations of unknown words are important strategies when deciphering SAT questions.

Next, we will introduce you to some puzzles that will help you to learn to build and deconstruct words.

Fun Quiz

1. What is the average acceptance rate at U.S. colleges and universities?
   a. 30 percent
   b. 40 percent
   c. 50 percent
   d. 60 percent
   e. 70 percent

2. What is the percentage of U.S. colleges and universities accepting 40 percent or less of applicants?
   a. 12 percent
   b. 6 percent
   c. 15 percent
   d. 21 percent
   e. 33 percent

3. According to college admissions officers, what is the most important factor in gaining admission to their college?
   a. SAT/ACT score
   b. Extracurricular activities
   c. Monetary gift to the alumni fund
   d. Academic performance, including courses taken
   e. Application essay

Answers

1. e
2. b
3. d

Source: The State of College Admission 2002–2003, National Association of College Admission Counselors.

SAT DECODER: LEARN TO BUILD AND DECONSTRUCT WORDS

HOW WORD CREATION PUZZLES, WORD WITHIN WORD PUZZLES, AND PHOBIA PUZZLES WILL HELP YOU RAISE YOUR SAT SCORE

On the verbal SAT you will have to try to decipher words that you do not know. If you cannot figure out the word from the context of the sentence or the passage, your only choice will be to try to break the word down into its prefix, word roots, and suffix. Word creation puzzles are wonderful practice for picking words apart because they ask you to build words from word pieces. Word within word puzzles ask you to find the pieces of the given words, and then to form new words based on those pieces. If you can build a word, then you can also take it apart. Once you know what a word root means, then you will be able to use it to build words or to take them apart. For example:

malediction	mal = bad	dict = tell, say, word
homogeneous	homo = same	gen = birth, race, kind
claustrophobia	cla/clo/clu = shut, close	phobia = fear of
postscript	post = after	scrip/scrib = write

Once you have pulled the words listed above into their pieces, you can come close to determining their definition. In fact, the SAT writers deliberately use words that can be pulled apart into roots and prefixes you probably know to see if you are comfortable with words, to see if you can play with words. You do not have to know every nuance of a word's definition in order to use the meanings of the pieces of the words to either keep or eliminate the words from the answer choices.

WORD CREATION PUZZLE INSTRUCTIONS

GOAL: To create as many words as possible from the prefixes, word roots, and suffixes listed. See if you can beat the total number of words created.

WHY: If you can build a word from its pieces, you can also pick it apart. Your ability to pick words into pieces will affect your score on the verbal SAT because you will be able to figure out an approximate meaning for many of the unknown words you encounter.

RULES: You may use each prefix, word root, or suffix as many times as you wish. Not all word parts have to be used. At least one word may be formed by combining word roots.

HINT: Look for familiar word roots first; then try to add prefixes and suffixes that make sense.

Word Creation Puzzle 1

Prefix	Word Root	Suffix
a = not	ten, tain = hold, reach	ual = of
in = in, on	ver = true	or = person who
pro = forward, toward	vert, vers = turn	y = inclined to
im = not	man = hand	ify = to make
pre = before	ject = throw	er = person who
re = again	pon, pos = place, put	ic = pertaining to
con = with	curr, curs = run	ile = pertaining to
com = with	fer = bear, carry	(t)ure = action or result
	gen = kind, race, birth	acity = state of being
	fort = strong	ant, ent = full of
	fac, fic, fec, fect = to make	sion, tion = that which is

_____
_____
_____
_____
_____
_____
_____

WORD WITHIN WORD PUZZLE INSTRUCTIONS

GOAL: To find as many "baby" words within the "mother" word as possible. Baby words must be created by using the letters in the mother word.

WHY: Words are made up of parts. If you can pull apart a word, there is a good chance that you will think of one or more words with one or more of the same parts. In fact, one of the ways in which SAT test writers enjoy themselves is to put a word on the SAT that they know you don't know. The test writers know that you know a word that either sounds or looks like the unknown word. If you make the connection between the words, then you can solve the question. Why the test writers think this is fun, I don't know, but consider what they do for a living!

RULES: Each word must be at least four letters long. No proper names or place names are allowed. *Hiker* and *hiked* are two separate and acceptable words; however, only one form of any verb or noun may be used. Thus in the case of *hiked* and *hiking,* you may only use one.

CLUE: Start by identifying all the roots in the words. Then see how many different words you can create using those roots as the base of a word. Only then should you move on to try other combinations of letters.

Word within Word Puzzle 1

frac·tious (frak´shəs), *adj.*

1. refractory or unruly: *a fractious animal that would not submit to the harness.*
2. readily angered; peevish; irritable; quarrelsome: *an incorrigibly fractious young man.*

Best score so far: 58

Word within Word Puzzle 2

com·pres·sion (kəm presh´ən), *n.*

1. the act of compressing; squeezing.
2. the state of being compressed; abridged.
3. the effect, result, or consequence of being compressed.
4. (in internal-combustion engines) the reduction in volume and increase of pressure of the air or combustible mixture in the cylinder prior to ignition, produced by the motion of the piston toward the cylinder head after intake.
5. reduction of the size of computer data by efficient storage.

Best score so far: 77

Word within Word Puzzle 3

fac·sim·i·le (fak sim´ə lē), *n., v.,* **-led, -le·ing,** *adj.*

1. an exact copy, as of a book, painting, or manuscript.
2. also called **fax** (*telecommunications*).
   a. a method or device for transmitting documents, drawings, photographs, or the like, by means of radio or telephone for exact reproduction elsewhere.
   b. an image transmitted by such a method.
3. dropout (def. 5).
   —*v.t.*
4. to reproduce in facsimile; make a facsimile of.
   —*adj.*
5. Also, **fax** (*telecommunications*).
   a. (of an image) copied by means of facsimile: *facsimile mail.*
   b. (of a method or device) used to produce a facsimile: *facsimile transmission.*

Best score so far: 47

PHOBIA PUZZLE INSTRUCTIONS

GOAL: To match each fear with its correct phobia name.

WHY: Phobia names are usually created from Greek or Latin roots. If you can match the fear with the phobia name, then you will know what all the roots in the phobia puzzle mean. And you will be able to surprise your friends and teachers with references to rare and odd phobias.

RULES: Each fear will match one phobia and vice versa. Some of the fears are similar in meaning, so look carefully at the roots in the list of phobias.

HINT: Start with phobias you recognize, and then look for word roots you recognize.

Phobia Puzzle 1

To Rachel, who is convinced she has readapoemaloudaphobia

Match the following fears with the name of their phobia!

Item	*Phobia*
1. ideas	a. gerontophobia
2. motion	b. sociophobia
3. stealing	c. traumatophobia
4. bicycles	d. philemaphobia
5. animals	e. ideophobia
6. the mind	f. kleptophobia
7. injury	g. necrophobia
8. poison	h. agrizoophobia
9. society	i. teratophobia
10. one thing	j. graphophobia
11. fire	k. zoophobia
12. old people	l. isolophobia
13. writing	m. polyphobia
14. wild animals	n. bacillophobia
15. symbolism	o. chorophobia
16. politics	p. symbolophobia
17. solitude	q. nucleomitophobia
18. germs	r. monophobia
19. kissing	s. kinetophobia
20. corpses	t. papyrophobia
21. symmetry	u. toxiphobia
22. monsters	v. cyclophobia
23. nuclear weapons	w. symmetrophobia
24. paper	x. pyrophobia
25. many things	y. politicophobia
26. dancing	z. psychophobia

END NOTE

Congratulations! You now have all the decoding tools you need to decipher the vocabulary on the new SAT. All you have to do is practice, both to master your new skills and to apply them to increasingly sophisticated words and puzzles. You are well on your way. In the next chapter we increase the difficulty level of the words and the puzzles to mirror the medium difficulty questions on the SAT. The first group of puzzles is designed to increase your vocabulary.

Fun Quiz

1. Which of the following statements was said by Mark Twain?

   I. The man who does not read good books has no advantage over the man who can't read them.

   II. My books are water; those of great geniuses are wine—everybody drinks water.

   III. I have been complimented many times and they always embarrass me; I always find that they have not said enough.

   IV. All you need in this life is ignorance and confidence, then success is sure.

   V. Man was made at the end of the week's work when God was tired.

      a. I and II
      b. II and III
      c. IV
      d. V
      e. All of the above

Answer

1. e

Chapter 4

PUZZLES TO INCREASE VOCABULARY

The crosswords from here on out will be harder: They're bigger in size, and there are no longer any two-letter words. If you made it through the first three crosswords in Chapter 1, then you're ready for these. Here are two tips that may help. First, never hesitate to open your dictionary if you see an unfamiliar word or a word you're not quite sure of. This is how we learn and improve at puzzles (and tests). Second, don't be afraid to set a tough puzzle aside and come back to it another time. It's amazing how often a clue that's impossibly difficult one day is blindingly obvious the next. It seems that sometimes our brains can work some overnight magic when it comes to figuring out tough answers.

Unfortunately, catastrophes and disasters occur. Some are caused by nature; some by people. There are plenty of words to describe these calamities, the situations where things go terribly wrong. Because in this world, it seems, there are plenty of things with "Destructive tendencies."

Crossword Puzzle 4
Destructive Tendencies

ACROSS

1. LA rap star born Tracy Morrow (hyph.)
5. With mouth wide open
10. Takeover of a government by force
14. Person who accomplishes things (anagram of "rode")
15. Use needle and thread to repair again
16. Odd green veggie used in gumbo
17. Totally destroy or eradicate
19. The Three Wise Men of Bethlehem, collectively
20. Actress Gershon of "Showgirls" (anagram of "gain")
21. Oscar _____ (hot dog making company)
22. Station for watching music videos and veejays
25. Massacre or slaughter of great numbers
29. Final year high schoolers (abbr.)
30. Sea captain who pursued Moby Dick
32. First showing of a movie or play
33. Ladies professional tennis star Monica
35. "I was, she was, you _____"
36. Class a year away from graduation (abbr.)
39. Threatening; foreboding; hinting at doom
42. State of great commotion or disturbance
44. One nickname for Edward
45. Study really, really hard
47. Baseball maneuver when trying to get to a base
48. Native Peruvians of the Andes
50. Place between your calf and thigh
51. Secret agent
54. Agreements; yesses
57. Common recipe direction amount (abbr.)
58. Follow someone as a detective would
60. Has lunch
62. Doesn't feel well (anagram of "sail")
63. Violent social or geological upheavals
69. White Greek cheese (anagram of "feat")
70. Very similar; almost the same
71. What a hammer hits
72. Noisy fight or skirmish
73. Last but not _____
74. Earthy material used in art class at school

DOWN

1. Two words you want to hear at your wedding
2. Inedible part of an ear of corn
3. Underwater animal that can be electric
4. Math class that might follow geometry (abbr.)
5. Indoor venue for sports or concerts
6. French movie star Depardieu (anagram of "regard")
7. _____ rule (generally speaking) (2 wds.)
8. Dog or cat one keeps at home
9. Mother sheep
10. _____ again? (Please repeat for me)
11. Gives approval to
12. Person trying to move you on
13. What socks, shoes, and mittens come in (anagram of "Paris")
18. _____-tac-toe
21. Electricity or water measuring devices (anagram of "merest")
22. Laborer who works with bricks or stones
23. _____ topic for a paper (school writing assignment)
24. Just true; well-founded
26. Just out of the wrapper, e.g.
27. Aid and _____ (assist a criminal)
28. Intellectual or spiritual guide
31. Actor Affleck
34. _____ studies (core middle school class)
36. Shoulder or hip, e.g.
37. Goes on a bike
38. What you do at night
40. Large, decorative vases (anagram of "runs")
41. Native Americans of the Midwest (anagram of "Cass")
43. Initials of a man's birthday celebrated every January
46. Actress West who said "Come up and see me, sometime"
49. Moves without being seen
51. Support group for a 4-star general
52. Nosy, snoopy person (anagram of "riper")
53. Black Sea port in the Ukraine
55. Musical direction meaning "be silent"
56. Initials logo of the Gateway Arch city
59. "Do as _____, not as..." (2 wds.)
61. 'N _____ (Justin Timberlake's band)
63. State west of Utah (abbr.)
64. Ginger _____ (soda)
65. Spanish word for "aunt"
66. "My Gal _____" (Erie Canal song)
67. "Mamma _____" (Broadway musical about Abba)
68. Cunning or wily

There's no satisfying some people. They want more. Always. More of everything; more even than they could possibly ever use. And there are words for these overly greedy people; the people who are disposed to saying: "Mine, all mine!"

Crossword Puzzle 5
Mine, All Mine!

ACROSS

1. "The Star-Spangled Banner" for one
7. Grow old
10. Enthusiastic; ardent
14. Grand _____ Island
15. Female parent
16. "Sleepless in Seattle" director Ephron
17. Greedy; covetous
19. Three-spot in a deck of cards
20. Armored military vehicle with a turret
21. Fake coin (anagram of "lugs")
22. The Mediterranean, e.g.
23. Large member of the American deer family
24. Generally awkward or incompetent
26. The "CSI" TV shows' network
29. Overly desirous of wealth or possessions
32. George Gershwin's brother (anagram of "air")
33. What the king sits on
36. Take to court to get money
37. Wet protection around a castle
38. Plow into the backside of another car (hyph.)
40. Acknowledgment of gratitude or esteem
42. Cable TV sports network
43. Quick trip into the swimming pool
45. "Skoal," "Cheers," and "Your health," e.g.
46. _____ general rule (usually) (2 wds.)
47. Having a craving or yearning for (with "of")
49. Month following November (abbr.)
50. Celestial constellation known as the Dragon
51. Bro or sis, for short
54. Suffix meaning a "person who practices"
56. Measures of thermal output (abbr. and anagram of "buts")
58. "_____ and the King of Siam"
59. Nike or Adidas product
61. Tending to eat and drink excessively
63. Common or proper word form
64. For each; for every
65. Friend of Pooh and Tigger
66. For fear that (anagram of "lets")
67. Sweet suffix for lemon or lime
68. Talks too much; babbles (anagram of "tapers")

DOWN

1. Lessen; diminish
2. Pertaining to warships (homonym of your belly button)
3. State your appreciation
4. "_____, the herald angels sing"

5. Music group that recorded The Beatles (anagram of "I me")
6. Apple computer products, for short
7. Totals; quantities
8. Dig a trench or groove (2 wds.)
9. Letters before "ens"
10. "Fee" for entering a poker hand (anagram of "nate")
11. Exceedingly eager; ravenous
12. Anger
13. 24-hour period
18. Tennis's "Nasty" Nastasie (reads like "I prevaricate")
22. Roads or lanes (abbr.)
25. _____ Rico (Caribbean country)
27. Actor Benjamin of "Law and Order"
28. Thoroughly fills or surfeits (anagram of "asset")
29. Food item that comes on a cob
30. "The _____ and only"
31. Seller of goods (variant spelling)
33. _____ lightly (be careful where you step)
34. Author Hermann of "Steppenwolf"
35. Inordinately greedy; predatory
37. Business graduate school degrees (anagram of "bams")
39. Incapacitated; turned off a PC function

41. Debt marker abbreviation
44. What you see on a TV or monitor
47. Banned chemical pesticide (abbr.)
48. Thoroughly beat in a battle (anagram of "tour")
51. Slang for the nose (anagram of "toons")
52. Accustom to hardship or difficulty
53. Ballplayers run toward these
55. Put into the mailbox
57. Part of a stairway or ladder
58. "Dragonwyck" novelist Seton
59. Comedian Tina Fey's TV skit show, for short
60. Tool used for weeding
61. Cumulative measure of your grades (abbr.)
62. "_____ the land of the free and..."

Most people like to live in attractive surroundings. They like to live in a home where they're proud to have other people come visit. So naturally there are a lot of words to describe the places where we live and how nice these places look. Because many people are tempted to say, "Our house (is a very, very, very fine house)."

Crossword Puzzle 6
Our House (Is a Very, Very, Very Fine House)

ACROSS

1. Do a picture in pencil
5. Endure
9. Small, wretched house
14. Knot or protuberance (anagram of "done")
15. Native Peruvian of the Andes
16. Popular zoo primate, "The Man of the Forest"
17. Having a sense of the beautiful
19. Tends to the baby
20. "Richard _____" (Shakespeare play)
21. You kneel on this
23. Wealth, riches, or affluence
28. Elaborately or sumptuously adorned
32. Clark Kent's girlfriend Lois
33. Lively or energetic spirit
35. Platter for carrying cafeteria food
36. Drag parachute (anagram of "rouged")
39. Famous women Gabor and Peron (anagram of "save")
41. Lash your shoelaces together
42. Capital city of Norway
44. Close cousin of Harvard and Princeton
46. Mediterranean, e.g.
49. Anthracite or bituminous material
51. Home decorating picture made of small, colored tiles
55. The guy who did it, in police talk
57. School group of parents and teachers (abbr.)
58. Bustle; fuss
59. Recess or small room in a house
61. One-story cottage
65. Thin puff or streak, as of smoke
67. Federal group in charge of security (abbr.)
68. Residence; dwelling; habitation
71. Maze that was home to the Minotaur
77. Extend a magazine subscription
78. Actor Hale or son Hale, Jr.
79. "_____ bambino" (Italian word for goodbye)
80. Budweiser products
81. DEA agent, for short
82. OK Corral marshal Wyatt

DOWN

1. Genetic messenger carrier (abbr.)
2. Fish eggs (anagram of "ore")
3. Commercials
4. More than just damp
5. _____ bed (laze about) (2 wds.)
6. Playful trick or prank
7. Chemistry or biology, e.g. (abbr.)
8. Bulletin board sticker
9. Bart Simpson's dad
10. Get one's bearings
11. Truck used for moving home furnishings
12. Final stopping point
13. T-shirt sizes for big people (abbr.)
18. Go in haste (homonym of a greeting word)
22. Polite negatory response to a lady (2 wds.)
23. Ancient
24. Average score for Tiger Woods
25. Spanish word for "one"
26. Danish plastic building block
27. Adam's Garden of Eden lady
29. Museum pieces, e.g.
30. _____ chi (exercise form)
31. What you see with
34. _____ League schools (Harvard, Princeton, etc.)
37. West Coast home of the college Trojans (abbr.)
38. Runs off to get married secretly
40. _____-mo (sports replay mode)
43. Cheerios cereal grain
45. "She is," in Spanish (anagram of "sate")
46. Exercise or beauty location
47. Fish type that might be electric
48. Part of the circumference of a circle
50. Where a scientist works, for short
52. DSL rival of Yahoo and MSN
53. Phrase you want to hear at a wedding (2 wds.)
54. Creature that moos
56. Kind of snow a skier likes
60. Aspects; vistas
62. To open a gated door (anagram of "braun")
63. Justin Timberlake's band
64. Needle-nosed fish
66. Plot and _____ (scheme)
68. Wall Street trader (anagram of "bar")
69. Hive dweller
70. "We're number _____!" (stadium chant)
72. State next to Mississippi (abbr.)
73. Frozen water
74. Vardalos of "My Big Fat Greek Wedding"
75. Black, sticky road-mending material
76. Jump like a bunny

Anagram Magic Square Puzzle 3

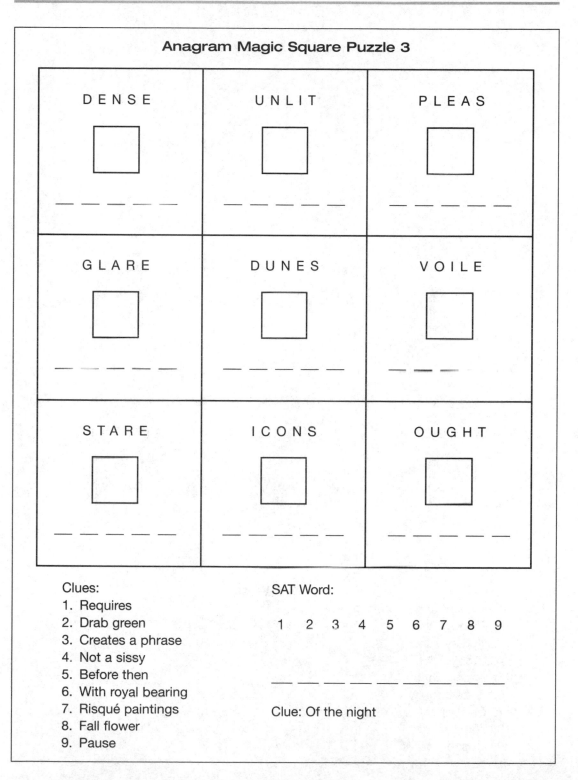

D E N S E

U N L I T

P L E A S

G L A R E

D U N E S

V O I L E

S T A R E

I C O N S

O U G H T

Clues:
1. Requires
2. Drab green
3. Creates a phrase
4. Not a sissy
5. Before then
6. With royal bearing
7. Risqué paintings
8. Fall flower
9. Pause

SAT Word:

1   2   3   4   5   6   7   8   9

_ _ _ _ _ _ _ _ _

Clue: Of the night

Anagram Magic Square Puzzle 4

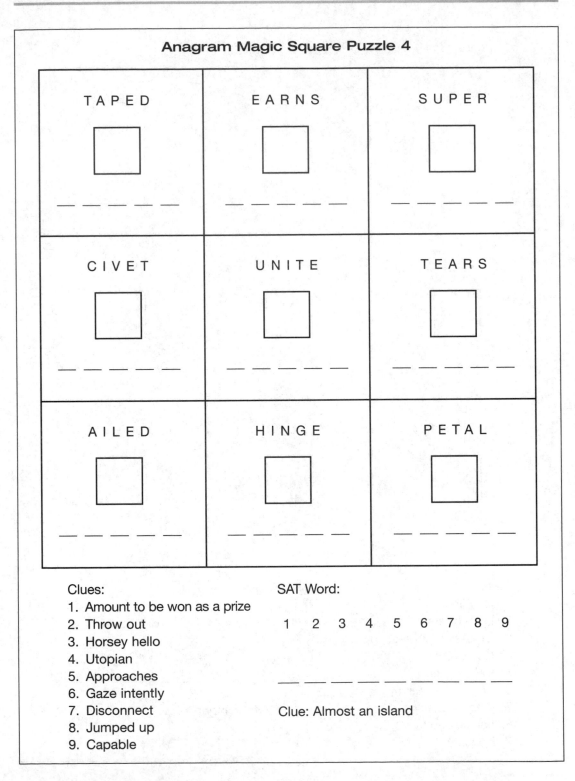

TAPED

EARNS

SUPER

CIVET

UNITE

TEARS

AILED

HINGE

PETAL

Clues:
1. Amount to be won as a prize
2. Throw out
3. Horsey hello
4. Utopian
5. Approaches
6. Gaze intently
7. Disconnect
8. Jumped up
9. Capable

SAT Word:

1   2   3   4   5   6   7   8   9

__ __ __ __ __ __ __ __ __

Clue: Almost an island

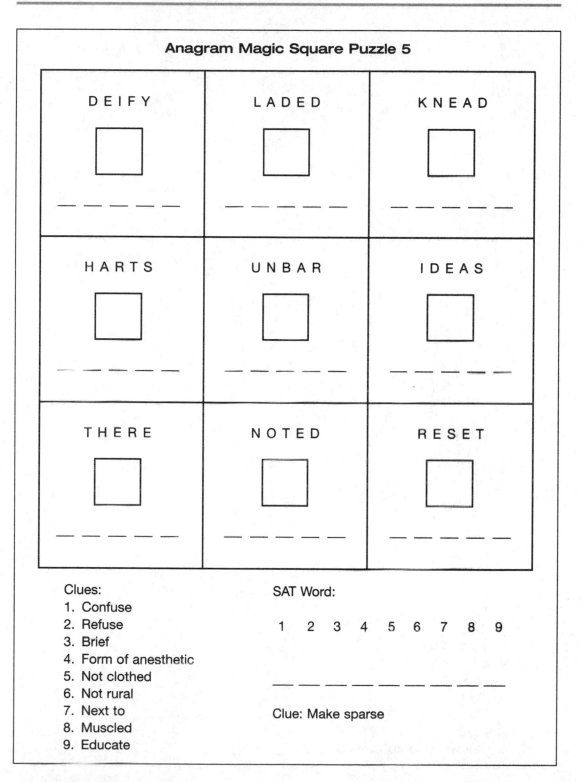

Anagram Magic Square Puzzle 5

DEIFY

LADED

KNEAD

HARTS

UNBAR

IDEAS

THERE

NOTED

RESET

Clues:
1. Confuse
2. Refuse
3. Brief
4. Form of anesthetic
5. Not clothed
6. Not rural
7. Next to
8. Muscled
9. Educate

SAT Word:

1   2   3   4   5   6   7   8   9

— — — — — — — — —

Clue: Make sparse

Anagram Magic Square Puzzle 6

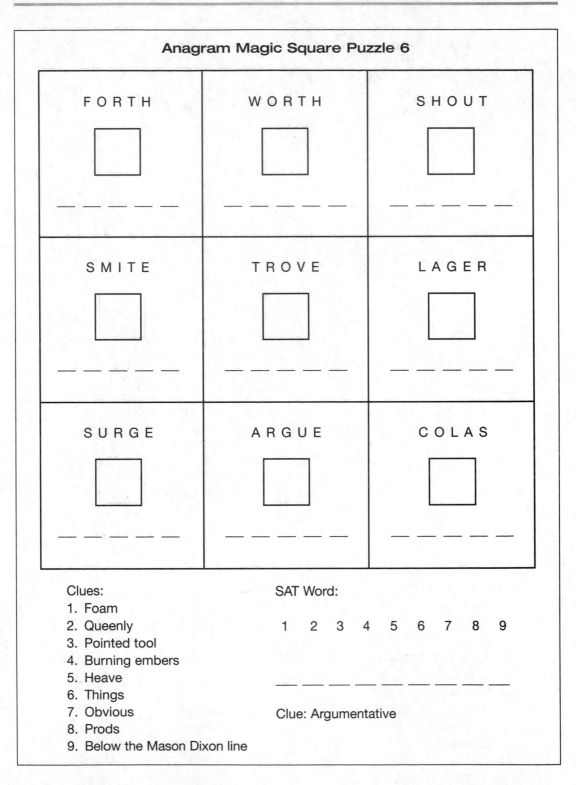

FORTH

WORTH

SHOUT

SMITE

TROVE

LAGER

SURGE

ARGUE

COLAS

Clues:
1. Foam
2. Queenly
3. Pointed tool
4. Burning embers
5. Heave
6. Things
7. Obvious
8. Prods
9. Below the Mason Dixon line

SAT Word:

1   2   3   4   5   6   7   8   9

— — — — — — — — —

Clue: Argumentative

Hidden Meanings Puzzle 3

som·ber (som´bər), *adj.*

1. _____(8) dark; shadowy; _____(5) lighted.
2. dark and _____(4), as color, or as things in respect to color.

vo·ca·tion (vō kā´shən), *n.*

1. a particular _____(10), business, or profession; _____(7).
2. a strong impulse or _____(11) to follow a particular activity or _____(6).

mal·e·dic·tion (mal´i dik´shən), *n.*

1. a _____(5); imprecation.
2. the _____(9) of a curse.

pro·voc·a·tive (prə vok´ə tiv), *adj.*

1. tending or serving to provoke; _____(8), stimulating, irritating, or _____(6).

vo·cif·er·ous (vō sif´ər əs), *adj.*

1. crying out noisily; _____(9).

in·frac·tion (in frak´shən), *n.*

1. _____(6); violation; _____(12).

sub·lime (sə blīm´), *adj., n., v.,* **-limed, -lim·ing.** —*adj.*

1. elevated or _____(5) in thought, language
2. _____(10) the mind with a sense of _____(8) or power; inspiring awe or _____(10).

ab·di·cate (ab´ di kāt´), *v.,* **-cat·ed, -cat·ing.** —*v.i.*

1. to _____(8) or relinquish a _____(6), right, power, claim, responsibility, or the like, especially in a _____(6) manner.

trans·gress (trans gres´, tranz-), —*v.i.*

1. to _____(7) a law, command, moral code, and so on; _____(6); sin.
2. to pass over or go _____(6) a limit or _____(8).

prod·i·gy (prod´i jē), *n., pl.* **-gies.**

1. a person, especially a child or young person, having _____(13) _____(6) or ability.
2. something wonderful or _____(9); a _____(6).

Hidden Meanings Puzzle 3 *(continued)*

4 LETTERS
DULL

5 LETTERS
CURSE
LOFTY
DIMLY

6 LETTERS
TALENT
VEXING
THRONE
OFFEND
BREACH
CAREER
WONDER
FORMAL
BEYOND

7 LETTERS
VIOLATE
CALLING

8 LETTERS
RENOUNCE
GLOOMILY
INCITING
GRANDEUR
BOUNDARY

9 LETTERS
UTTERANCE
MARVELOUS
CLAMOROUS

10 LETTERS
IMPRESSING
VENERATION
OCCUPATION

11 LETTERS
INCLINATION

12 LETTERS
INFRINGEMENT

13 LETTERS
EXTRAORDINARY

Some words in a particular definition will be interchangeable.

Hidden Meanings Puzzle 4

post·script (pōst′ skript′, pōs′ -), *n.*

1. a paragraph, phrase, and the like, added to a _____(6) that has already been _____(9) and signed by the _____(6).

sanc·ti·fy (sangk′ tə fī′), *v.t.,* **-fied, -fy·ing.**

1. to make _____(4); set apart as sacred; _____(10).
2. to _____(6) or free from sin.

quest (kwest), *n.*

1. a search or _____(7) made in order to find or _____(6) something.
2. Medieval romance, an adventurous _____(10) undertaken by a knight or knights to secure or _____(7) something.

ex·e·cra·ble (ek′ si krə bəl), *adj.*

1. utterly _____(10); abominable; _____(9).

pro·lix (prō liks′, prō′liks), *adj.*

1. extended to great, _____(11), or _____(7) length; long and wordy.

quer·u·lous (kwer′ə ləs, kwer′yə-), *adj.*

1. full of _____(10); complaining.
2. characterized by or uttered in complaint; _____(7).

em·pa·thy (em′pə thē), *n.*

1. the intellectual identification with or _____(9) experiencing of the _____(8), thoughts, or _____(9) of another.

dis·par·age (di spar′ij), *v.t.,* **-aged, -ag·ing.**

1. to speak of or treat slightingly; _____(9); _____(8).
2. to bring reproach upon or _____(9); lower the estimation of.

cir·cu·i·tous (sər kyōō′i təs), *adj.*

1. _____(10); not direct.

dif·fi·dent (dif′i dənt), *adj.*

1. lacking _____(10) in one's own ability, _____(5), or fitness; _____(5); shy.
2. restrained or _____(8) in manner, conduct, and so on.

Hidden Meanings Puzzle 4 *(continued)*

4 LETTERS
HOLY

5 LETTERS
TIMID
WORTH

6 LETTERS
OBTAIN
WRITER
PURIFY
LETTER

7 LETTERS
PEEVISH
ACHIEVE
TEDIOUS
PURSUIT

8 LETTERS
FEELINGS
BELITTLE
RESERVED

9 LETTERS
ABHORRENT
DISCREDIT
VICARIOUS
CONCLUDED
ATTITUDES
DEPRECATE

10 LETTERS
COMPLAINTS
EXPEDITION
CONFIDENCE
CONSECRATE
ROUNDABOUT
DETESTABLE

11 LETTERS
UNNECESSARY

Some words in a particular definition will be interchangeable.

Hidden Meanings Puzzle 5

vil·i·fy (vil´ ə fī´), *v.t.*, **-fied, -fy·ing.**
1. to speak ill of; _____(6); _____(7).

whet (hwet, wet), *v.*, **-ted, -ting,** *n.* —*v.t.*
1. to _____(7) (a knife, tool, etc.) by grinding or _____(8).
2. to make _____(4) or eager; _____(9).

spurn (spûrn), *v.t.*
1. to reject with _____(7); _____(5).
2. to treat with _____(8); _____(7).

vi·brant (vī´brənt), *adj.*
1. moving to and fro _____(7); _____(9).
2. vibrating so as to produce _____(5), as a string.

a·bridge (ə brij´), *v.t.*, **-ed, -ing.**
1. to _____(7) by _____(8) while retaining the basic content.
2. to reduce or lessen in _____(8), scope, authority, and so on; _____(8).

daunt (dônt, dänt), *v.t.*
1. to overcome with _____(4); _____(10).
2. to lessen the _____(7) of; _____(10).

ob·scu·ri·ty (əb skyŏŏr´i tē), *n., pl.* **-ties.**
1. the state or _____(7) of being _____(7).

dis·crep·an·cy (di skrep´ən sē), *n., pl.* **-cies.**
1. the state or quality of being discrepant; _____(10); _____(13).

hy·poc·ri·sy (hi pok´rə sē), *n., pl.* **-sies.**
1. a _____(8) of having a _____(8) character, _____(5) or _____(9) beliefs or principles, and the like, that one does not really _____(7).

bane (bān), *n.*
1. a person or thing that _____(5) or _____(6).

Hidden Meanings Puzzle 5 *(continued)*

4 LETTERS
FEAR
KEEN

5 LETTERS
SCORN
RUINS
SOUND
MORAL

6 LETTERS
DEFAME
SPOILS

7 LETTERS
DESPISE
QUALITY
UNKNOWN
DISDAIN
SHARPEN
POSSESS
RAPIDLY
SLANDER
SHORTEN
COURAGE

8 LETTERS
PRETENSE
DIMINISH
VIRTUOUS
CONTEMPT
FRICTION
DURATION
OMISSION

9 LETTERS
STIMULATE
RELIGIOUS
VIBRATING

10 LETTERS
DISHEARTEN
INTIMIDATE
DIFFERENCE

13 LETTERS
INCONSISTENCY

Some words in a particular definition will be interchangeable.

Hidden Meanings Puzzle 6

myr·i·ad (mir´ē əd), *n.*

1. a very _____(5) or _____(12) great _____(6) of persons or things.

de·plete (di plēt´), *v.t.*, **-plet·ed, -plet·ing.**

1. to _____(8) seriously or _____(7) the _____(9) or supply of.

am·biv·a·lence (am biv´ə ləns), *n.*

1. uncertainty or _____(11), especially when caused by _____(9) to make a _____(6) or by a _____(12) desire to say or do two opposite or _____(11) things.

flour·ish (flûr´ish, flur´-), *v.i.*

1. to be in a _____(8) state; _____(6).
2. to be in its or in one's _____(5); to be at the height of fame, _____(10), influence, and so on.
3. to be successful; _____(7).

dis·tend (di stend´), *v.t.*, *v.i.*

1. to _____(6) by stretching, as something hollow or _____(7).
2. to _____(6) in all directions; expand; _____(5).

pe·riph·er·al (pə rif´ər əl), *adj.*

1. pertaining to, situated in, or constituting the _____(9).
2. concerned with relatively minor, _____(10), or _____(11) aspects of the subject in question.

gar·ner (gär´nər), *v.t.*

1. to gather or _____(7) in or as if in a granary or other _____(7) place.
2. to get; _____(7); _____(4).

tran·sient (tran´shənt, -zhənt, -zē ənt), *adj.*

1. not lasting, _____(8), or _____(9); _____(10).
2. lasting only a _____(5) time; existing _____(7); _____(9).

vir·u·lent (vir´yə lənt, vir´ə-), *adj.*

1. actively _____(9); intensely _____(7).
2. *Medical:* highly infective; _____(9) or deadly.

sty·mie (stī´mē), *n.*, *v.*, **-mied, -mie·ing.** *—n.*

1. a _____(9) or problem presenting such _____(12) as to discourage or _____(6) any attempt to deal with or _____(7) it.

Hidden Meanings Puzzle 6 *(continued)*

4 LETTERS	7 LETTERS	9 LETTERS
EARN	BRIEFLY	PERMANENT
	PROSPER	INABILITY
5 LETTERS	NOXIOUS	MALIGNANT
SWELL	STORAGE	TEMPORARY
SHORT	RESOLVE	ABUNDANCE
PRIME	ELASTIC	SITUATION
LARGE	EXHAUST	POISONOUS
	DEPOSIT	PERIPHERY
6 LETTERS	ACQUIRE	
SPREAD		10 LETTERS
THRIVE	8 LETTERS	EXCELLENCE
NUMBER	ENDURING	TRANSITORY
LARGER	VIGOROUS	IRRELEVANT
DEFEAT	DECREASE	
CHOICE		11 LETTERS
		CONFLICTING
		FLUCTUATION
		SUPERFICIAL
		12 LETTERS
		DIFFICULTIES
		SIMULTANEOUS
		INDEFINITELY

Some words in a particular definition will be interchangeable.

Hidden Meanings Puzzle 7

fraud·u·lent (frô´jə lənt), *adj.*

1. characterized by, involving, or _____(10) from _____(5), as actions, _____(10), methods, or gains.
2. given to or using fraud, as a person; _____(8); _____(9).

ob·du·rate (ob´dŏŏ rit, -dyŏŏ-), *adj.*

1. _____(7) by _____(10), pity, or tender feelings; stubborn; _____(10).

re·cal·ci·trant (ri kal´si trənt), *adj.*

1. resisting _____(9) or control; not obedient or _____(9); _____(10).
2. _____(4) to deal with, _____(6), or operate.

e·phem·er·al (i fem´ər əl), *adj.*

1. lasting a _____(4) short time; short-lived; _____(10).

sa·lu·bri·ous (sə lŏŏ´brē əs), *adj.*

1. _____(9) to or _____(9) health; healthful.

cor·rob·o·rate (*v.* kə rob´ə rāt; *adj.* kə rob´ər it), *v.*, **-rat·ed, -rat·ing,** *adj.* —*v.t.*

1. to make _____(7); to _____(7).

mu·nif·i·cent (myŏŏ nif´ə sənt), *adj.*

1. extremely _____(7) in _____(6); very _____(8).

par·si·mo·ny (pär´ sə mō´nē), *n.*

1. extreme or _____(9) economy or _____(9); _____(10).

sur·rep·ti·tious (sûr´əp tish´əs), *adj.*

1. _____(8), done, made, and so on, by _____(7); secret or _____(12); _____(11).

dis·so·nance (dis´ə nəns), *n.*

1. _____(12) or harsh sound; _____(7); _____(9).
2. *Music:* a _____(12) combination of tones conventionally accepted as being in a state of unrest and needing _____(10).

Hidden Meanings Puzzle 7 *(continued)*

4 LETTERS	8 LETTERS	10 LETTERS
HARD	OBTAINED	STINGINESS
VERY	CHEATING	ENTERPRISE
	GENEROUS	UNYIELDING
5 LETTERS		TRANSITORY
FRAUD	9 LETTERS	COMPLETION
	EXCESSIVE	PERSUASION
6 LETTERS	FAVORABLE	PROCEEDING
GIVING	CACOPHONY	REFRACTORY
MANAGE	DISHONEST	
	COMPLIANT	11 LETTERS
7 LETTERS	PROMOTING	CLANDESTINE
CERTAIN	FRUGALITY	
STEALTH	AUTHORITY	12 LETTERS
UNMOVED		SIMULTANEOUS
LIBERAL		UNAUTHORIZED
DISCORD		INHARMONIOUS
CONFIRM		

Some words in a particular definition will be interchangeable.

Hidden Meanings Puzzle 8

ab·ste·mi·ous (ab stē′mē əs), *adj.*

1. sparing or _____(8) in eating and drinking; _____(9) in diet.
2. characterized by _____(10).

sub·or·di·nate (*adj., n.* sə bôr′dn it; *v.* sə bôr′dn āt′), *adj., n., v.,* **-nat·ed, -nat·ing. —***adj.*

1. placed in or _____(9) to a _____(5) order or _____(4).
2. of less importance; _____(9).
3. subject to or under the authority of a _____(8).
4. _____(11) or inferior.

re·gress (*v.* ri gres′; *n.* rē′gres), *v.i.*

1. to move _____(8); to go _____(4).
2. to _____(6) to an earlier or less _____(8) state or form.

frac·tious (frak′shəs), *adj.*

1. _____(10) or unruly.
2. readily angered; _____(7); irritable; _____(11).

ob·se·qui·ous (əb sē′kwē əs), *adj.*

1. characterized by or showing _____(7) complaisance or _____(9); _____(7).

e·man·ci·pate (i man′sə pāt′), *v.t.,* **-pat·ed, -pat·ing.**

1. to free from _____(9), _____(9), or the like.
2. to free (a slave) from _____(7).

in·gen·u·ous (in jen′yo͞o əs), *adj.*

1. free from reserve, restraint, or _____(13); _____(6); sincere.
2. artless; _____(8); _____(5).

su·per·cil·i·ous (so͞o′pər sil′ē əs), *adj.*

1. haughtily _____(10) or contemptuous, as a person or a facial _____(10).

con·viv·i·al (kən viv′ē əl), *adj.*

1. _____(8); agreeable.
2. fond of _____(8), drinking, and merry company; _____(6).
3. of or befitting a feast; _____(7).

co·a·lesce (kē′ə les′), *v.,* **-lesced, -lesc·ing. —***v.i.*

1. to grow _____(8) or into one _____(4).
2. to _____(5) so as to form one _____(9).

Hidden Meanings Puzzle 8 *(continued)*

4 LETTERS
BACK
MASS
RANK

5 LETTERS
NAIVE
LOWER
UNITE

6 LETTERS
CANDID
JOVIAL
REVERT

7 LETTERS
FAWNING
FESTIVE
PEEVISH
BONDAGE
SERVILE

8 LETTERS
INNOCENT
BACKWARD
TOGETHER
SUPERIOR
FRIENDLY
MODERATE
ADVANCED
FEASTING

9 LETTERS
SECONDARY
COMMUNITY
RESTRAINT
BELONGING
TEMPERATE
INFLUENCE

10 LETTERS
DISDAINFUL
REFRACTORY
ABSTINENCE
EXPRESSION

11 LETTERS
SUBSERVIENT
QUARRELSOME

13 LETTERS
DISSIMULATION

Some words in a particular definition will be interchangeable.

END NOTE

If a man empties his purse into his head, no man can take it away from him. An investment in knowledge always pays the best interest. Ben Franklin

How did you do? The puzzles and the vocabulary were more challenging in this chapter than in the previous chapters. You now know more vocabulary words than you did before you began the chapter, you are more comfortable trying to figure out what unknown words mean, and you are getting better at word puzzles. Don't worry if you were not able to finish every puzzle. Most students have to leave some squares or blanks empty here and there. Sometimes all you need is a little distance. Try going back on a different day to puzzles you have not been able to complete. Many times you will be able to finish the puzzle then.

Fun Quiz

1. How many students in the class of 2003 took the SAT?
   a. 1.4 million
   b. 2.3 million
   c. 1.6 million
   d. 1.0 million
   e. 0.8 million

2. What percentage of students taking the SATs will be the first in their household to attend college?
   a. 27 percent
   b. 43 percent
   c. 38 percent
   d. 19 percent
   e. 22 percent

3. The number of minorities taking the SAT was at an all-time high in 2002–2003. What percentage of students taking the SAT are minorities?
   a. 26 percent
   b. 18 percent
   c. 42 percent
   d. 51 percent
   e. 36 percent

4. Why does the College Board (the association that owns the SAT) say it has added writing to the new SAT?*
   a. It will give students practice for their application essays.

b. It will help colleges make better admissions and placement decisions.

c. It will provide colleges with a writing sample that hasn't been rewritten by parents, teachers, guidance counselors, and private college counselors.

d. It will make the SATs longer and more difficult.

e. It will give colleges a handwriting sample that they can have analyzed for personality traits.

Answers

1. a

2. c

3. e

4. b

* Collegeboard.org

Source: The State of College Admission 2002–2003, National Association of College Admissions Counselors.

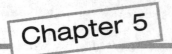

Chapter 5

WORD CONNECTION PUZZLES

Human history has seen a lot of brilliant individuals. We have invented many words for them: genius, savant, sage. And there are plenty of other words to describe: Brainy people.

Crossword Puzzle 7
Brainy People

ACROSS

1. _____ as a tack (really brainy)
6. Top 40 hit
10. Killer whale (anagram of "Cora")
14. Weird (sounds like a Great Lake)
15. "O Brother, Where Art _____" (George Clooney film)
16. Suffix meaning "composed of"
17. Mentally developed at a very young age
19. Smallest of a litter of puppies
20. Partner word of
21. The _____ degree (ultimate)
23. Wildebeest (anagram of "gun")
24. Singer Turner of "Private Dancer"
28. "_____ it there" (offer to shake hands)
30. Be better batters in a baseball game
32. Really brainy
34. Baby dog or seal
36. Fashion designer Geoffrey
37. Go on _____ (walk the grounds for security's sake)
39. Use oars
41. "Incredible Hulk" director Lee
42. Cleverly inventive or resourceful
45. Chevy Suburban or Tahoe, for short (abbr.)
47. Elevated railways, for short
48. Come out from a hiding place
52. Scatter or sprinkle about
54. Water and dirt mixed together
56. Outdoor spot shaded by trees and bushes
57. _____ toward (going in that direction)
59. "The _____ and the Pendulum" (Poe)
61. Takes a chair
62. Competed in a foot race
63. Perfect score for a gymnast
65. Shipboard distress signal
67. Give off gamma rays (anagram of "time")
69. Having keenness of insight or understanding
75. Not physically strong
76. Cream-filled black cookie
77. Broadcast a TV show
78. James Bond's first movie villain (2 wds.)
79. Actors Cruise and Hanks
80. Gets introduced to someone for the first time

DOWN

1. Month before Oct. (abbr.)
2. Not him
3. "I am, he is, you _____"
4. Guitarist Ocasek of The Cars
5. Unskilled laborer (anagram of "nape")
6. Get all riled or agitated (2 wds.)
7. "So that's what's going on!"
8. Word form that can be common or proper
9. Hearty or enthusiastic pleasure
10. "_____ the land of the free, and the home..."
11. Make scratchy or abrasive
12. Craftiness or guile
13. Really clever or shrewd
18. Slang for a police officer
22. Center of activity or commerce
24. Common recipe amount (abbr.)
25. "_____ a little teapot..." (2 wds.)
26. _____ Turner's Rebellion (1831 uprising)
27. Showed up at the door
29. Appears at last (2 wds.)
31. Previews designed to arouse your curiosity
33. 2000 pounds
35. Hawaiian food made of taro roots
38. Big shirt size (abbr.)
40. Grievous affliction or trouble
43. Common American tree
44. "Kill Bill" actress Thurman
45. Mississippi riverboat, once
46. From the planet next to Neptune
49. Stat for a baseball batter
50. Obtained
51. Words or sounds of hesitation
52. Brainy in practical matters
53. Moist or damp, e.g.
55. Night spots for dancers
58. Train station or stop
60. Digit at the end of your foot
64. Emperor who fiddled while Rome burned
66. Junk e-mail taken collectively
68. Boxing win declared by the ref (abbr.)
70. Michael Stipe's band
71. Finish putting on your shoes
72. Anger, rage
73. Dog or cat doctor, for short
74. Actors Begley and Begley, Jr.

We often need a little push to get us going, some help from a friend or a teacher. It's not that we can't get started; it's just that sometimes we're a little slow and need someone to say: "Come on! Let's get going."

Crossword Puzzle 8
Come On! Let's Get Going

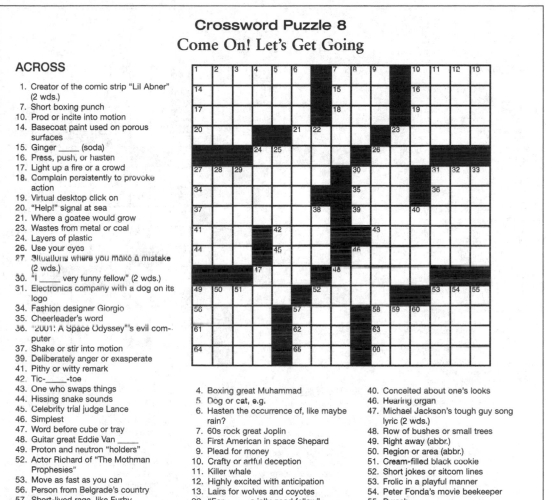

ACROSS

1. Creator of the comic strip "Lil Abner" (2 wds.)
7. Short boxing punch
10. Prod or incite into motion
14. Basecoat paint used on porous surfaces
15. Ginger _____ (soda)
16. Press, push, or hasten
17. Light up a fire or a crowd
18. Complain persistently to provoke action
19. Virtual desktop click on
20. "Help!" signal at sea
21. Where a goatee would grow
23. Wastes from metal or coal
24. Layers of plastic
26. Use your eyes
27. Situations where you make a mistake (2 wds.)
30. "I _____ very funny fellow" (2 wds.)
31. Electronics company with a dog on its logo
34. Fashion designer Giorgio
35. Cheerleader's word
36. "2001: A Space Odyssey"'s evil computer
37. Shake or stir into motion
39. Deliberately anger or exasperate
41. Pithy or witty remark
42. Tic-_____-toe
43. One who swaps things
44. Hissing snake sounds
45. Celebrity trial judge Lance
46. Simplest
47. Word before cube or tray
48. Guitar great Eddie Van _____
49. Proton and neutron "holders"
52. Actor Richard of "The Mothman Prophesies"
53. Move as fast as you can
56. Person from Belgrade's country
57. Short-lived rage, like Furby
58. Wheedle or coax with flattery
61. Length times width product
62. Scrambled breakfast item
63. Actor Val of "Batman Forever"
64. Poke into action
65. Suffix meaning "inhabitants"
66. Running at an angle downhill

DOWN

1. Take it or leave it store sign (2 wds.)
2. Plastic building block from Denmark
3. Sealed food containers
4. Boxing great Muhammad
5. Dog or cat, e.g.
6. Hasten the occurrence of, like maybe rain?
7. 60s rock great Joplin
8. First American in space Shepard
9. Plead for money
10. Crafty or artful deception
11. Killer whale
12. Highly excited with anticipation
13. Lairs for wolves and coyotes
22. "For _____ a jolly good fellow"
23. Undersea "mount"
24. Junior year take on what this book is all about!
25. Nut jobs; wackos
26. Wiseacres (2 wds.)
27. Terms of politeness for women
28. Latin words meaning "therefore"
29. Actor Jimmy of "Attack of the Clones"
30. French surrealist painter Jean
31. _____ Island (state)
32. Layered desserts
33. Warn everybody
38. Prefix meaning "environment"
40. Conceited about one's looks
46. Hearing organ
47. Michael Jackson's tough guy song lyric (2 wds.)
48. Row of bushes or small trees
49. Right away (abbr.)
50. Region or area (abbr.)
51. Cream-filled black cookie
52. Short jokes or sitcom lines
53. Frolic in a playful manner
54. Peter Fonda's movie beekeeper
55. Dweeb
57. Cost of professional services
59. Be unwell
60. Ben Affleck's costar and former squeeze, for short

Every once in a while you come across something you wish you hadn't—something really disgusting or gross, a situation, a smell, or something that's just plain bad. There are some words to describe these moments—the ones that make you want to say: "P-U, that's yucky!"

Crossword Puzzle 9
P-U, That's Yucky!

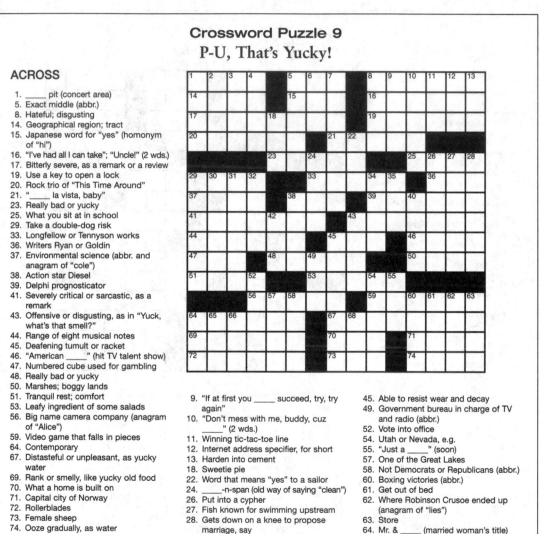

ACROSS

1. _____ pit (concert area)
5. Exact middle (abbr.)
8. Hateful; disgusting
14. Geographical region; tract
15. Japanese word for "yes" (homonym of "hi")
16. "I've had all I can take"; "Uncle!" (2 wds.)
17. Bitterly severe, as a remark or a review
19. Use a key to open a lock
20. Rock trio of "This Time Around"
21. "_____ la vista, baby"
23. Really bad or yucky
25. What you sit in at school
29. Take a double-dog risk
33. Longfellow or Tennyson works
36. Writers Ryan or Goldin
37. Environmental science (abbr. and anagram of "cole")
38. Action star Diesel
39. Delphi prognosticator
41. Severely critical or sarcastic, as a remark
43. Offensive or disgusting, as in "Yuck, what's that smell?"
44. Range of eight musical notes
45. Deafening tumult or racket
46. "American _____" (hit TV talent show)
47. Numbered cube used for gambling
48. Really bad or yucky
50. Marshes; boggy lands
51. Tranquil rest; comfort
53. Leafy ingredient of some salads
56. Big name camera company (anagram of "Alice")
59. Video game that falls in pieces
64. Contemporary
67. Distasteful or unpleasant, as yucky water
69. Rank or smelly, like yucky old food
70. What a home is built on
71. Capital city of Norway
72. Rollerblades
73. Female sheep
74. Ooze gradually, as water

DOWN

1. Alan Alda's long run TV sitcom
2. Killer whale (anagram of "Cora")
3. Actor Penn of "Mystic River"
4. Headwear
5. Beijing's country
6. Get brown from the sun
7. "Exactly, dude!" (hyph. wd.)
8. Burden
9. "If at first you _____ succeed, try, try again"
10. "Don't mess with me, buddy, cuz _____" (2 wds.)
11. Winning tic-tac-toe line
12. Internet address specifier, for short
13. Harden into cement
18. Sweetie pie
22. Word that means "yes" to a sailor
24. _____-n-span (old way of saying "clean")
26. Put into a cypher
27. Fish known for swimming upstream
28. Gets down on a knee to propose marriage, say
29. Break or solve a cypher
30. Another name for the locust tree
31. Postal carriers' paths
32. Joy Adamson's "Born Free" lioness
34. Earth's satellite
35. _____ Lanka (Asian country)
38. Watch a movie or show, e.g.
40. "Yeah, like, I would really do something like that" (2 wds.)
42. Big New Deal dam project (abbr.)
43. Africa's longest river
45. Able to resist wear and decay
49. Government bureau in charge of TV and radio (abbr.)
52. Vote into office
54. Utah or Nevada, e.g.
55. "Just a _____" (soon)
57. One of the Great Lakes
58. Not Democrats or Republicans (abbr.)
60. Boxing victories (abbr.)
61. Get out of bed
62. Where Robinson Crusoe ended up (anagram of "lies")
63. Store
64. Mr. & _____ (married woman's title)
65. Tree that grows acorns
66. Genetic "cargo carrier"
68. Use oars

Quotation Puzzle 3

1H	2J	3E	4B	5C	6A	7L	8F		9E	10K	11H	12A		13E	14H		15A
16E	17B		18F	19I	20D		21K	22D	23C	24J		25I	26B	27H		28I	29E
30L	31G		32A	33L	34J		35L	36G	37B	38E		39D	40C	41G	42J	43K	44B
45E	46H		47I	48B	49F	50A	51J	52D	53G	54K		55C	56L	57B	58F	59D	60H
	61F	62J	63B	64I	65A	66G	67K	68L	69C	70H	71E						

Clues:

A. Ren's bud

$$\overline{65}\ \overline{12}\ \overline{6}\ \overline{50}\ \overline{32}\ \overline{15}$$

B. Not genuine, authentic, or true

$$\overline{57}\ \overline{63}\ \overline{37}\ \overline{48}\ \overline{44}\ \overline{26}\ \overline{17}\ \overline{4}$$

C. The Lone Star State

$$\overline{5}\ \overline{23}\ \overline{40}\ \overline{55}\ \overline{69}$$

D. Chompers

$$\overline{20}\ \overline{59}\ \overline{39}\ \overline{52}\ \overline{22}$$

E. Giant sequoias

$$\overline{38}\ \overline{3}\ \overline{13}\ \overline{9}\ \overline{29}\ \overline{16}\ \overline{71}\ \overline{45}$$

F. Not right

$$\overline{58}\ \overline{61}\ \overline{49}\ \overline{8}\ \overline{18}$$

G. Hammers, saws, screwdrivers, etc.

$$\overline{31}\ \overline{36}\ \overline{41}\ \overline{53}\ \overline{66}$$

H. Divider of the Northern and Southern Hemispheres

$$\overline{70}\ \overline{1}\ \overline{27}\ \overline{11}\ \overline{46}\ \overline{14}\ \overline{60}$$

I. Quietest one of the Seven Dwarfs

$$\overline{28}\ \overline{64}\ \overline{47}\ \overline{19}\ \overline{25}$$

J. Extreme poverty; destitution

$$\overline{51}\ \overline{62}\ \overline{24}\ \overline{2}\ \overline{42}\ \overline{34}$$

K. Like gum or caramel

$$\overline{43}\ \overline{10}\ \overline{67}\ \overline{21}\ \overline{54}$$

L. Bugs, like your little sister or brother

$$\overline{33}\ \overline{56}\ \overline{30}\ \overline{7}\ \overline{35}\ \overline{68}$$

Quotation Puzzle 4

1A	2I	3L	4C	■	5B	6A	7C	8L	9K	10F	11I	12H	■	13L	14E	15C	16B
17G	■	18D	19B	20G	21L	■	22F	23A	24E	25J	■	26L	27F	28B	29J	■	30H
■	31G	32A	33H	34C	■	35L	36G	37I	■	38I	■	39I	40G	41H	■	42L	43A
44M	■	45K	46C	47B	48J	49E	■	50J	51B	52C	53D	■	54C	55E	56J	57K	■
58J	59E	60B	61G	■	62M	■	63H	64B	65M	■	66D	67J	68K	■	69M	■	70A
71D	72F	73K	■	74F	75J	76D	77B	■	78M	79A	80K	81C	82L	83G	■		

Clues:

A. China-born director of Travolta's "Broken Arrow" (2 wds.)

$\overline{70}\ \overline{79}\ \overline{23}\ \overline{43}\ \overline{1}\ \overline{6}\ \overline{32}$

B. TV talk show host and sometime actress (2 wds.)

$\overline{16}\ \overline{51}\ \overline{5}\ \overline{28}\ \overline{19}\ \overline{77}\ \overline{64}\ \overline{60}\ \overline{47}$

C. Zealous; ardent; impassioned

$\overline{46}\ \overline{81}\ \overline{4}\ \overline{15}\ \overline{52}\ \overline{34}\ \overline{7}\ \overline{54}$

D. Poet T. S. of "The Wasteland"

$\overline{53}\ \overline{76}\ \overline{66}\ \overline{71}\ \overline{18}$

E. Weighing a lot

$\overline{55}\ \overline{24}\ \overline{59}\ \overline{14}\ \overline{49}$

F. Fiddle with software code or electronic parts

$\overline{22}\ \overline{74}\ \overline{10}\ \overline{27}\ \overline{72}$

G. Term of address for the king

$\overline{20}\ \overline{40}\ \overline{31}\ \overline{61}\ \overline{83}\ \overline{36}\ \overline{17}$

H. Takes a stroll

$\overline{41}\ \overline{30}\ \overline{63}\ \overline{33}\ \overline{12}$

I. Travels by ship

$\overline{37}\ \overline{38}\ \overline{2}\ \overline{39}\ \overline{11}$

J. Reckless boldness; rashness

$\overline{67}\ \overline{56}\ \overline{58}\ \overline{29}\ \overline{48}\ \overline{75}\ \overline{50}\ \overline{25}$

K. Old Faithful, to name one

$\overline{80}\ \overline{73}\ \overline{57}\ \overline{68}\ \overline{45}\ \overline{9}$

L. Leave one's country to settle in another

$\overline{21}\ \overline{26}\ \overline{35}\ \overline{8}\ \overline{82}\ \overline{42}\ \overline{3}\ \overline{13}$

M. Emmy, Oscar, or Grammy, e.g.

$\overline{69}\ \overline{65}\ \overline{62}\ \overline{78}\ \overline{44}$

Quotation Puzzle 5

1B		2G	3F	4E	5A	6C		7D	8E	9F		10G	11B		12A	13D	14C
15F	16H	17G	18C	19H	20B		21B	22D	23C	24H	25F	26C	27F	28A	29B		30E
31D	32B	33A		34F	35C		36E	37A	38B	39D	40G	41C	42E	43D	44B		45G
46D	47E	48H		49H	50A	51G	52G	53B									

Clues:

A. Particularly sharp or astute

$\overline{12}\ \overline{33}\ \overline{28}\ \overline{5}\ \overline{50}\ \overline{37}$

B. Clever inventiveness

$\overline{1}\ \overline{44}\ \overline{20}\ \overline{29}\ \overline{53}\ \overline{38}\ \overline{21}\ \overline{32}\ \overline{11}$

C. Frugal; skillful at managing money

$\overline{23}\ \overline{14}\ \overline{6}\ \overline{18}\ \overline{26}\ \overline{41}\ \overline{35}$

D. Expressing much in few words

$\overline{7}\ \overline{46}\ \overline{13}\ \overline{43}\ \overline{22}\ \overline{31}\ \overline{39}$

E. Roger Ebert critique

$\overline{47}\ \overline{8}\ \overline{4}\ \overline{42}\ \overline{36}\ \overline{30}$

F. Home theater controller

$\overline{25}\ \overline{3}\ \overline{34}\ \overline{15}\ \overline{9}\ \overline{27}$

G. Karl Malone's NBA nickname

$\overline{10}\ \overline{40}\ \overline{52}\ \overline{17}\ \overline{45}\ \overline{51}\ \overline{2}$

H. Keepsake

$\overline{49}\ \overline{16}\ \overline{48}\ \overline{24}\ \overline{19}$

| **Cryptofamily Puzzle 5** | **Cryptofamily Puzzle 6** |
| That's Ancient History | Anger Mismanagement |

| SXBKS | MJGOUMQCA |
| *DATED* | *INFURIATE* |

| XHNMXCN | MUA |

| MXNWGKVKS | AJUQKA |

| DRYDJKBK | MJFAJNA |

| YIQKHXGGIXBK | WUDBDPA |

| DIBSXBKS | ATWRDVA |

| DJS-LXYMCDGKS | GOEA |

| QHDBDBVQK | UQKA |

| XGNKYBHXJ | NAACYA |

| XGBKNKSKGB | SUMNCRA |

| QHDPKGCBDH | SDMR |

| DHCPCGXJ | GOUL |

| XGBCAIK | DOCUQKA |

| ECGBXPK | CDUEAJC |

| DIBFDSKS | QJJDL |

Cryptofamily Puzzle 7
Oh, No, You Don't!

N B X H N L D O
R E S T R A I N

C P D J

C B H H B N

Q L G T B N

U L N

I P O X H N L D O

I W N U

I P O C D O B

I N L G T

X H N D I H W N B

N B X H N D I H

X L O I H D P O

C P N U D E

H Q Z L N H

X H M G D B

Cryptofamily Puzzle 8
I'm in My Right Mind

O W P G T D W Y
R A T I O N A L

K W D V

S O H F V D P

Y H B G F

E W Y W D B V F

C H F G B G T H K

O V W K T D W E Y V

K W R W B G T H K

K V D K G E Y V

U G K V

S V O B V S P G N V

B T R D G I W D P

F G K B V O D G D R

K W S G V D P

B T J V O V D P

Cryptofamily Puzzle 9
On the Road to Nowhere

S A L V Q A F
M E A N D E R

O A L J A

O L V Q A F

Q A J P L C A

N P E N L E

R O A F J A

C O P R C

R V L M A

R M A O

R O L I

G X P H

G X F M R G F A O

G W F H

R T P F L H

C O P V A

Cryptofamily Puzzle 10
We Need an Exorcism Here

R H X E Y O H G
D I A B O L I C

G A V W O

R W I H O H K P

J P Y V O H K P

H U Z W A U X O

Y J A W H K P

K X Q X U H G

E X A E X A Y V K

E W K Q H X O

Z W A X O

Z W A Y G H Y V K

H U P V N X U

K X I X J W

I H G H Y V K

F Y O Z H K P

Cryptofamily Puzzle 11
It Was the Biggest Fish You Ever Saw!

W C P M C E Q
S T R E T C H

M V X B B M P X C M

Q T Z M P D U K J S M

J I A K X C M

F X B I J A T

U G M P E Q X P B M

U G M P W C X C M

X B B P X I L J S M

M I I U D K M

W M I W X C J U I X K J S M

M F D M K K J W Q

M F D P U J L M P

M I Q X I E M

X F Z K J A T

G X P I J W Q

Cryptofamily Puzzle 12
Duty Calls

X U Z W M U I N
V A L I D A T E

S Z N M Y N

X J F T B D J P

S P J V W L N

U F I B N Q I W T U I N

L F C L I U Q I W U I N

T J V V W I

T J P P J C J P U I N

J C Z W Y U I N

T N P I W D O

X J K

T J Q I P U T I

L K N U P

U X N P

X N P W D O

Cryptofamily Puzzle 13
Life Is Good

A G J P X Y
B L I T H E

K I F Y M F Y Y

E Y A C R I J F

W B F J U X P G O

G J U X P X Y I F P Y E

Y T D A Y F I R P

N C O M D G

Y A D G G J Y R P

Y M M Y F H Y W K Y R P

H J H I K J C D W

P F J D Q B X I R P

N D A J G I R P

Y T D G P I P J C R

I R J Q I P Y E

H J U C F C D W

Cryptofamily Puzzle 14
The Lowest of the Low

M G E M F C P V C H V
S U B S T A N D A R D

E C M A

W K N N K P

Y G N E S A

Q D P K E S A

K H V Q P C H Z

I S A E Q C P

B G S D C H

Q P O A H Q K H

N A V Q K W H A

M Y K V V Z

F H Q F A

W S Q W Y A

E C P C S

Y C W R P A Z A V

Cryptofamily Puzzle 15
The Winner's Circle

E Q U K O Z D V
D O M I N A T E

A V M D

H Q O Y I V L

U Z M D V L

J L V R Z K P

M I L U Q I O D

Q R V L H Q U V

D L K I U J F

E V W V Z D

L Q I D

M I A E I V

R Z O Y I K M F

D L Z O M H V O E

V B H V V E

M I L J Z M M

Cryptofamily Puzzle 16
Waste Not, Want Not

H K L S F
S P A R E

F A X S L B L W L Q X

C I K S E B C Z F Q X

K S E Z C W L O

O L B C H N

H K F Q Z X N S C P X

F A V F H H

W O G X

P L X

H G K F S P O G E G H

H G S K O G H

K S E O C A

H G S P F C X

C I I E Z F S L X F

S F Z G Q Z L Q X

Groupie Puzzle 3	**Groupie Puzzle 4**
G E T S I T N E A R D I	Y E F I R N
D _ _ _ N _ _ _ _ _ _ _	_ I _ _ R _
R V E U L A N	W E E D J E E L B
_ N _ _ _ E _	B E _ _ _ _ _ _ _
T E D I E V C E F	D A D R E N O
_ _ F _ _ T _ _ _	_ _ O _ N _ _
G N S U A L H I	M L Y A E S
L _ _ _ _ I _ _	_ L _ _ _ E
N A W E K E	T H I G A E N N C N
_ E _ _ E _	_ _ C _ _ _ _ I _ _
H I O S A N O N D E N	G L L E E N A S I A T C O R R A E
_ _ _ A _ _ _ I _ _	S _ _ _ _ _ _ _ _ _
	E _ _ _ _ _ _ _
Groupie Phrase	
P M A E O M C T T T R A A H A S E S E	*Groupie Phrase*
_ _ M _ _ _ _ _ _ _ _ _	S I T E D D O L L E S R K
_ _ _ _ E _ _ _	_ _ _ S _ _ _ _ _ _ _ _ L _

END NOTE

You are on your way! As you did the last group of word connections puzzles, you learned two important concepts about solving verbal questions on the SAT. Very few high school students will know every word used on the SAT. Therefore, you must have a strategy for solving questions that include words you do not know. The puzzles you just completed helped you to create associations among words based on word connotations. If you can determine a word's general connotation, then you can use that knowledge to help you determine the correct answer on the verbal questions you are unsure of.

The other important concept you learned with this last batch of puzzles has to do with word associations. All the puzzles in this batch contain words that are related to one another. You will not remember all the distinctions among the words, but if you see one of the words in this batch on a test, you will remember that it was in a puzzle with, for example, other "friendly" words. That information will be enough to allow you to keep or eliminate answer choices.

Next, we are going to learn about word roots. You will put words together and take them apart. Just for fun, you will match a list of strange fears with their matching phobias by figuring out the meaning of the word roots.

Fun Quiz

1. One of the following schools is not a "seven sister." Which one is it?
   a. Vassar College
   b. Smith College
   c. Mills College
   d. Bryn Mawr College
   e. Wellesley College

2. All of the following colleges are affiliated with the Catholic church except:
   a. University of Notre Dame
   b. Lehigh University
   c. College of the Holy Cross
   d. Boston College
   e. University of Scranton

3. Which school is the training ground for the U.S. Army's future leaders?

   a. The Citadel

   b. The U.S. Naval Academy at Annapolis

   c. NORAD

   d. West Point

   e. College of William and Mary

Answers

1. c. Mills College

2. b. Lehigh University

3. d. West Point

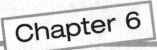

BACK TO THE ROOTS PUZZLES

We're all human, so we all make mistakes. That means we have plenty of opportunities to think of ways to make up for the things we've done wrong. Here are some words to help you say: "I am so sorry."

Crossword Puzzle 10
I Am So Sorry

ACROSS

1. Tool used for cutting wood
4. Jail or prison units
9. Foam; lather; soapy water
13. Make a mistake
14. Atlantic, Pacific and Indian, e.g.
16. _____ cadabra (magician's word)
17. Genuinely sorry or regretful
19. Crazy as a _____ (bird name)
20. Zero; zilch; none
21. Sincerely sorry and wanting to make up for
23. Tilted; slanted geometrically (anagram of "Glenda")
26. _____-cone (icy dessert)
27. Coffee alternative
28. Showing sincere remorse
31. Small child
33. Put to work
34. "Go on, get outta here!"
36. Big name in cameras
40. Take a break; take a load off
42. Bother someone persistently, as a problem (2 wds.)
44. The Abominable Snowman
45. State in Northeastern India (anagram of "amass")
47. Add one's share to the mix (2 wds.)
49. State directly west of Kansas (abbr.)
50. Washington, DC deal maker (anagram of "lop")
52. Feeling sorry and wanting to make up for something
54. Standard cooking recipe amount (abbr.)
57. Tree that grows acorns
59. The World _____ (baseball championship)
60. Feeling disappointed or humiliated
64. Permit; allow
65. Lead singer of rock music's U2
66. Genuinely sorry for having done wrong
70. Wisest of the "Star Wars" Jedi knights
71. No longer in fashion
72. Baseball rules decider, for short
73. Number, datum, piece of info, for short
74. _____ Wrap (kitchen coverer)
75. _____ Vegas, Nevada

DOWN

1. Large body of water
2. French painter Jean (anagram of "rap")
3. State of not being right that'll make you say "sorry"
4. Picnic iced drinks holders
5. Medicine's electrocardiogram test (abbr.)
6. Look with a sideways or oblique glance
7. _____ for class (tardy)
8. Small cuts with scissors
9. Complement of pepper
10. German submarine from World War II (hyph.)
11. Talk on endlessly and boringly
12. Yearly Christmas present deliverer
15. Smell or aroma
18. Song or tune (anagram of "till")
22. Secluded corner of a room
23. Make of Japanese car
24. Organs you smell with
25. You roll these hoping to make a 7
29. Fall into a _____ (get snared)
30. Really, really enjoy (2 wds.)
32. What a small child plays with
35. Liverpool pal or buddy
37. Misleading; fraudulent
38. Make up for one's sins or errors
39. Scottish skirts for men
41. Hit the floor with a cane
43. What food is stored in; cans
46. Firmly secure a ship with ropes
48. Big name in sweeps week television ratings
51. Landed proprieter in Scotland
53. Pine, maple, beech, or cedar, e.g.
54. Frozen yogurt stores, for short
55. Fire a gun
56. Bamboo-eating zoo favorite from China
58. Joints between your ankles and hips
61. Farm animal much like a sheep
62. English actress Thompson
63. You enter a room through this
67. Vitamin label abbreviation (anagram of "rad")
68. Actress Thurman
69. These were played before CDs were invented

Some people are passive or shy; some just don't feel the need to say very much. Here are some words to describe those people; the silent types, the guys who, when you describe them to your friends, you might say, "He's the quiet type."

Crossword Puzzle 11
He's the Quiet Type

ACROSS

1. Police officer
4. Wagers
8. This reportedly makes waste
13. Gorilla or chimpanzee, e.g.
14. Length times width product
15. People found in "People Magazine"
16. The quiet type keeps to himself, he's often shy and _____
18. Most ready to eat, as fruit
19. Puts one's clothes on
20. Portable trough for carrying bricks
21. _____ Lee pastries
22. He's reluctant to speak or join conversations; he's _____
27. Computer or typewriter features
31. Largest of the continents
32. Particularly appropriate
35. Kinda
36. Straight and limp, as hair
37. The quiet type is very abrupt in manner; you might call him _____
39. The quiet type says what he means in few words; he's usually pretty _____
42. Downhill snow racing vehicle
43. Stringed instrument smaller than a cello
45. Primary color
46. Soft, yellow cheese
47. In the middle
49. The quiet type is often reluctant to speak; he's _____
51. Women's magazine with a French name
55. Close relative of CTRL or ESC
56. Sofa or recliner softener
59. Opposite of most dangerous
63. The quiet type is known for verbal brevity; his comments are usually _____
64. Allows
65. Fitzgerald of jazz singing fame
66. Coffee or teacup handle
67. The quiet type's sentences are brief and pithy; his comments are _____
68. Actors Alda or Arkin
69. Sylvester Stallone's nickname

DOWN

1. Jack, queen, and king, e.g.
2. "The Barber of Seville," to name one
3. Actor Falk or Fonda
4. Jail cell features
5. One of the Great Lakes
6. Fingers or toes numbers
7. Droop
8. Fictional girl of Switzerland
9. Mountain you might find 8 Down on
10. Use your eyes
11. Ted Turner's Superstation
12. Ballpark figure (abbr.)
15. Close relatives of gators
17. Author Dinesen of "Out of Africa"
20. Got upset like Bart Simpson (3 wds.)
22. Tit for _____ (equal measure)
23. Mineral base for a body powder
24. Aviation company with a Pittsburgh hub
25. Washing machine cycle
26. Without a stitch of clothing on
28. Abbreviation found after a lawyer's name
29. "Yes, I mean _____!"
30. Stop something bad from happening
32. More capable of doing a task
33. Excessively proper person
34. Pull on repeatedly (2 wds.)
38. Prefix meaning "half"
40. Bull fight cheer
41. Word meaning "no" in Scotland
44. Hairy cousin from "The Addams Family"
47. These'll help keep your pants up
48. Maker of grape or orange soda
50. Social group of the same rank
52. Groups waiting at the movie box office
53. In one's own neighborhood
54. Way of getting in
56. Choose; select or pick
57. West Coast home of the college Bruins
58. Read over hastily
59. "_____ Bilko" (Steve Martin movie)
60. "You _____ My Sunshine"
61. A long way away
62. Navy rank below lieutenant (abbr.)
63. The Mediterranean, e.g.

We occasionally run into people who are too hyper and really need to calm down. We need some words to say to these people, words for when you want to say, "Dude, you need some chill pills."

Crossword Puzzle 12
Chill Pills

ACROSS

1. _____ one's time (wait)
5. Presidential hopefuls Gore and Smith
8. Calm down to a peaceful state
14. Neutron and proton "container"
15. _____ de Janeiro (Brazilian city)
16. "Songs in A Minor" singer Keys
17. Makes milder or less severe
19. Sways to and fro; flutters
20. Situation that just won't work (hyph.) (anagram of "goon")
21. Zero; none; zilch
22. Bring to a state of peace or calm
26. Calm someone down by using conciliatory gestures
30. Word referring to property (anagram of "raylet")
31. How Miss Piggy refers to herself
32. White winter stuff
33. Monte _____, Monaco (anagram of "coral")
34. Loafs about
36. Mother deer
37. Make easier to endure; lessen
40. Suffix with novel, real, or social
43. "Old MacDonald had a farm, _____"
44. Kid's comeback to "are so" (2 wds.)
48. Big gooey mess of stuff
50. "Before," to Shakespeare
51. Spanish fleet that Sir Francis Drake fought
52. Soften someone's feelings or temper
54. Lessened or relieved; mitigated
55. Daniel in the lion's _____ (Biblical story)
56. Goad into action
57. Retard or prevent from going faster (2 wds.)
60. Calming down, like a baby
65. Heat up pottery in the kiln again
66. You hear with this
67. Largest of the continents
68. Ease the blow; make less hard
69. Dr. of rap music fame
70. Kind of haircut or rug

DOWN

1. Sound a sheep makes
2. "_____ not a joke!"
3. MS-_____ (PC operating system)
4. Relative of the ostrich
5. Large merchant ship or fleet of ships
6. "My _____" (address for a feudal lord)
7. Just average (hyph.)
8. Lion or tiger's "hand"
9. Singer Davis of "Blame It on Me"
10. Study of the obligations of citizens (or Honda cars!)
11. Reykjavik's country
12. Tree of the pine family or its wood
13. Library sections for young adults (abbr.)
18. Nobel literature winner named France from France
22. Part of the circumference of a circle
23. Vegetable that comes in a pod
24. Average score for Tiger Woods
25. Fitzgerald of jazz singing fame
26. Disease prevented by Dr. Jonas Salk's vaccine
27. Country singer McCann of "Down Came a Blackbird"
28. As well as
29. Mother sheep
31. _____ theater (film venue)
34. Wary; suspicious
35. Up and coming movie actress word
38. "Gladly," to Shakespeare (anagram of "file")
39. English actress Thompson
40. Company initials seen on many personal computers
41. Traffic sign shorthand for "don't go fast"
42. Dressed down or a gave a talking to (2 wds.)
45. "No" vote word
46. "_____ on a Grecian Urn" (Keats)
47. Small amount
49. Bungled the chance to make the play (2 wds.)
51. He ran against George W. Bush in 2000 (2 wds.)
53. Get used to by repeated use
54. Cheering and noisy, like a crowded stadium
56. Not bought new, like many a car
57. Classes following junior years (abbr.)
58. "Titanic's" DiCaprio, to his friends
59. Writing utensil
61. Owns; possesses
62. Suffix meaning "belonging to"
63. Actress Vardalos of "My Big Fat Greek Wedding"
64. Fast joke or laugh provoker

Word Creation Puzzle 2

Prefix	Root	Suffix
ex = out	domin = lord, master	at = to make
ante = before	arch = rule, govern	or = person who
re = again	cad, cas, cid = fall	(a)ence = full of
in(m) = in, on	grad, gress = step, go	ile, le = pertaining to
pro = forward, toward	stat, stab = stand	ive = like
counter = against	tract = draw	e(y) = inclined to
at = to, forward	ced, cess = yield, go	(i)ate = to make
di = two	ag, act = do, act	(a)ent = full of
an = without	plic = fold, bend	ous = full of
com = with	voc, vok = call	il, al = pertaining to
matri = mother	mater, matr = mother	ity, it, ty = state of being
		(s)(t)ion = that which is
		uate = to make
		a(i)ble = able

Best score so far: 53

_____

_____

_____

_____

_____

_____

_____

_____

Word Creation Puzzle 3

Prefix	*Root*	*Suffix*
se = separate	sequ, secut = follow	(a)tive = like
im = into, on, in	mut = change	(a)tion = that which is
pre = before	nat = born	ial = pertaining to
con = together	bas, base = low	ory = a place for
de = away from	cred = low	tude = state of
trans = across	curr, curs = run	ment = result or action
in = into, on, in	fac, fact, fect, fic = do, make	al, el = pertaining to
multi = many	mult = many	able = able
	ven, vent = come	y = full of
	sum, summ,	ible = able
	sume, sumpt = take	ious = full of
	far = law, right	(t)ate = one who
		ile = pertaining to
		ent = full of
		e = we don't know but a lot of words have it!

Best score so far: 44

_____

_____

_____

_____

_____

_____

_____

_____

_____

Word Creation Puzzle 4

Prefix	Root	Suffix
in = in, on, upon	ac, acr, acri, acerb = sharp	(u)(i)ous = full of
re = again, back	aud, audit = hear	(a)ible = able
a = without	doc, doct, docu = teach	ence = full of
com = with, together	string, strict = bind	ory = denoting spaces
pre = before	omni = all	ile = pertaining to
con = with, together	trud, trus = to push, to shove	ate = to make
pro = forward, in favor of	vac, evacu = empty	ity = state of being
	sci = to know	ure = result
	phil = love	(e)or = person who
	soph = wisdom	ine = pertaining to
	mon = to warn	(a)ent = full of
		ment = result or action
		ry = business or occupation
		(a)(s)(t)ion = that which is

Best score so far: 30

_____

_____

_____

_____

_____

_____

_____

_____

_____

_____

Word Creation Puzzle 5

Prefix

sub = under

in = not

de = away

con = with

ad = forward, toward

into = into

pre = before

re = again

Root

bibl = book

chron = time

chrom = color

cosm = world

dorm, dormi = sleep

miss, mit = send

nov, novel = new

scrib, script = write

apt = fit

volv, volut = to roll

graph, gram = writing

Suffix

ology = study of

ic = having some
        characteristic of

(t)ory = denoted place
        (sometimes)

(i)tude = state of

ty = quality or state

(a)(s)tion = that which is

ant = full of

(a)tic = pertaining to

y = full of

ical = pertaining to

ice = indicating state or
        quality

Best score so far: 31

_____

_____

_____

_____

_____

_____

_____

_____

_____

_____

Cryptofamily Puzzle 17
Give Me More!

L R T O Q I Q V Q N A
A C Q U I S I T I V E

L R M A

L N L E Q R Q F O I

R F N A V F O I

H A I Q E F O I

E L C L R Q F O I

A D N Q F O I

W S O V V F D F O I

W E A A H K

R E L N A

M O D W A E

K A L E D

K A D

L C C A V Q V A

C L I I Q F D L V A

Cryptofamily Puzzle 18
Takeaways

H E E P W G O H M W
A B B R E V I A T E

U J O M

B N E M P H Y M

I W I N Y M

I O J O C O B F

Y U C I W C B W

I W Y O J H M W

W L Y Z N I W

W V W Y M

H Z Z W G O H M W

W P H I O Y H M W

W L M O P Q H M W

W L Q N P K H M W

U F Z O M W P H M W

H E P O I K W

Cryptofamily Puzzle 19
You Look Marvelous

P I G R K N R B Q
R A V I S H I N G

C I R P

A X I W V X J W K

X Z L W R K R V X

P I U R I B V

H I Q B R C R Y X B V

T R B K J H X

P X C R B X U

X F X Q I B V

Q F I H J P J W K

Y N R Y

K W A F R H X

P X K O F X B U X B V

O W F Y N P R V W U R B J W K

K V I V W X K L W X

Cryptofamily Puzzle 20
You Said It!

N G C A R A E Y P
P L A T I T U D E

C Y C I P

F C H R F

N D S Q P D W

C N O S D R K F

P N R I D C F

F S A A S

K G S I C J

P N R A O P A

C H R S F

A D E R K F

W C J C G R A T

B G R B O P

W D S F R Y P

Y R B A E F

Cryptofamily Puzzle 21
Protest Types

P Q Q P D C D M
O P P O N E N T

K S Y Y S K C D M

D P D L P D H P A I S Y M

Q A P M C Y M E D M

Y C L M E A S E D

Q E A M S Y E D

Y C Q E A E M S Y M

Y L W S Y I E M S L

I E J L P D M C D M

K C M A E L M P A

L P D Y L S C D M S P B Y
P V T C L M P A

B D L P D G C D M S P D E J S Y M

V P W C I S E D

K S Y Y C D M S C D M

H E L M S P D E J S Y M

Cryptofamily Puzzle 22
Keep Your Eyes Peeled

J I G H B D H
O B S E R V E

G T W M

R J M P N J B

G F B D H Z

G T B F N P M P U H

B H T J M M J P N H B

G T J F N

L H B F G H

X W L H

X W K V

J X E H

B H W O

P M D P X P E W N H

G L H T N W N H

K P N M H G G

Cryptofamily Puzzle 23
I Care. I Really, Really Care

N G T D U Q
A R D E N T

D L L F V A J D

A U Q D U V D

A E X N V V A R U D T

Y D N H R F V

J D S D E D U Q

X N V V A R U N Q D

G N X Q F G R F V

D W V Q N Q A W

A U L H N E D T

A E X D Q F R F V

Q D E X D G N E D U Q N H

J R H N Q A H D

E D H R T G N E N Q A W

L N U N Q A W N H

Cryptofamily Puzzle 24
The Professor Speaks

J Q V M F C
D I C T U M

P U D B J Q W S G F Y B M

U N Y M S U Q V D W

Q C H Y U Q S F E

Y U F J Q M Y

S U D M S U Z

Y W S G F Y B V Y

J Q J D V M Q V

V S B X S W F M Y J

H U S O S F B J

J S P C D M Q V

E D P D V Q S F E

Q B J S V M U Q B D M Y

Y E S M Y U Q V

D U V D B Y

Cryptofamily Puzzle 25
Be My Friend

W E U W C E R V L K
G R E G A R I O U S

C M M C I H U

W U Z R C H

C X L Z D L H C E

D V E G R C H

D V L E O U V L K

D V Z W U Z R C H

I H R O B U

A B R H C Z O B E V A R D

I U Z R W Z

N R Z K V P U

C P R C I H U

M U H R D R O V L K

K C Z W L R Z U

F V D L H C E

Cryptofamily Puzzle 26
Get Away from Me

W O I I F G X Y O
B E L L I C O S E

U L O M L I X L Y

Q I X X K

B F Y G X M B Q Z S

G Q Z S Q Z A O M X L Y

Q W M Q Y F T O

W M L Y U L O

D Q I O T X I O Z S

N O M Z F G F X L Y

Z O K Q M F X L Y

G X Z S O P N S L X L Y

G X P W Q S F T O

F Z G X M M F C F W I O

K M Q G S F X L Y

J Q L C J S H

Cryptofamily Puzzle 27
Do It!

W X Q S G W G J H J Q
P R E C I P I T A T E

H A G J H J Q

Q E A Q E N Q X

J H E J H D G B Q

S H P T D Q

G E S G J Q

W X T I T Z Q

H S J G I H J Q

W X T N

S T Q X S Q

A T H N

S T E V S X G W J

G A E G J Q

Q E P T G E

H X T Y V Q

Cryptofamily Puzzle 28
Put-downs

K Y T H W M Y H Q
C A S T I G A T E

K F W P Q

Q G K Z S W Y H Q

P W T S Q T L Q K H

K F Y T H W T Q

P Q X W M S Y H Q

P W T L Y S Y M Q

A Y I J Y T H Q

S Q L S W I Y X P

K Q X T D S Q

S Q L S Z Y K F

I Y A W M X

O W A W N E

J Q A W H H A Q

J Q S Y H Q

Phobia Puzzle 2

Match the following fears with the name of their phobia.

Item	Phobia
1. people	a. androphobia
2. numbers	b. logophobia
3. words	c. vestiphobia
4. sound	d. bibliophobia
5. airsickness	e. didaskaleinophobia
6. men	f. graphophobia
7. loneliness	g. chromophobia
8. books	h. philophobia
9. plants	i. acousticophobia
10. meat	j. pharmacophobia
11. color	k. hedonophobia
12. crowds	l. phobophobia
13. school	m. anthrophobia
14. church	n. autophobia
15. writing	o. theophobia
16. pleasure	p. aeronausiphobia
17. large objects	q. venustaphobia
18. drugs	r. botanophobia
19. love	s. traumatophobia
20. fear	t. arithmophobia
21. light	u. tachophobia
22. speed	v. carnophobia
23. God	w. photophobia
24. injury	x. megalophobia
25. clothing	y. ecclesiophobia
26. beautiful women	z. demophobia

Phobia Puzzle 3

Match the following fears with the name of their phobia.

Item	*Phobia*
1. motion	a. thalassophobia
2. doctors, hospitals	b. acerbophobia
3. body odor	c. obesophobia
4. cold things	d. anginophobia
5. sourness	e. onomatophobia
6. sunlight	f. potophobia
7. the left	g. odontophobia
8. disease	h. bromidrophobia
9. sea	i. phalacrophobia
10. drink	j. arachnophobia
11. freedom	k. hematophobia
12. large objects	l. pathophobia
13. names	m. sinistrophobia
14. everything	n. mnemophobia
15. gaining weight	o. peccatiphobia
16. wine	p. iatrophobia
17. spiders	q. textophobia
18. heart problems	r. megalophobia
19. gravity	s. heliophobia
20. blood	t. uranophobia
21. teeth	u. panphobia
22. sin	v. dromophobia
23. baldness	w. barophobia
24. memories	x. oenophobia
25. fabric	y. eleutherophobia
26. heaven	z. frigophobia

END NOTE

We hope that learning word roots was fun! Word roots are the keys that will help you unlock the mystery around unknown words on the SAT. Word roots will give you enough information so that you will be able to eliminate or keep an answer choice on the SAT. Word roots will provide you with connotations so that you can get the gist of an important sentence in a reading passage. You do not have to be afraid of unknown words anymore. Words can be deciphered, their clues unlocked, piece by piece, so that you can determine the meaning of a word you do not know. What wonderful keys to take with you to unlock the SAT.

Fun Quiz

1. Match the quotation with its speaker:
   a. Never express yourself more clearly than you think.
   b. Everybody is ignorant, only in different subjects.
   c. It is not enough to have a good mind. The main thing is to use it well.
   d. There is no substitute for hard work.
   e. Grasp the subject; the words will follow.

      1. Will Rogers
      2. Thomas Edison
      3. Cato
      4. Niels Bohr
      5. René Descartes

Answers
1. Will Rogers, b.
2. Thomas Edison, d.
3. Cato, e.
4. Niels Bohr, a.
5. René Descartes, c.

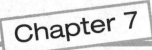

Chapter 7

VOCABULARY BUILDING PUZZLES

Traditionally, quotation puzzles come with a twist. They contain an "acrostic": the first letters of the answer words spell out a secret message. Sound hard? It's really not. This can actually make solving the puzzle easier. If you get stuck elsewhere, you can always read down the answer list and search for words or names. We'll give you another hint as well. The first two puzzles in this section have an acrostic that tells what the quotes are about; the final three spell out the author's name and the theme of the quote. As always, don't be afraid to consult your dictionary if you're not sure of an answer. Some of the vocabulary words here are hard. And take heart. Professional editors think that if you can figure out as few as three of the answer words (two in a shorter quote), you can solve the entire puzzle by working back and forth.

Quotation Puzzle 6

1I	2D		3A	4B	5D		6E	7C	8J	9I		10A	11I	12H	13C	14G	
15A	16G	17C	18L	19B	20F	21H	22D		23B	24K	25L	26F		27F	28E	29C	30J
	31E	32C	33F		34I	35G	36H	37E	38F		39E		40L	41C	42A	43J	44K
	45G	46F	47I	48L	49J	50H		51G	52H	53E	54J	55C	56F		57H	58A	59D
60B	61F		62L	63A		64E	65B	66J	67A	68H	69K	70L		71C	72A	73D	74I
75F	76L	77K	78G		79G	80A	81F	82I									

Clues:

A. Feelings of strong dislike; ill will

$\overline{10}\ \overline{63}\ \overline{42}\ \overline{80}\ \overline{58}\ \overline{15}\ \overline{72}\ \overline{67}\ \overline{3}$

B. Former MTV veejay "Downtown" Julie

$\overline{19}\ \overline{65}\ \overline{4}\ \overline{23}\ \overline{60}$

C. The Sooner State

$\overline{13}\ \overline{71}\ \overline{55}\ \overline{7}\ \overline{41}\ \overline{32}\ \overline{17}\ \overline{29}$

D. Make into a single unit

$\overline{5}\ \overline{73}\ \overline{59}\ \overline{2}\ \overline{22}$

E. Nervous and jumpy

$\overline{53}\ \overline{64}\ \overline{39}\ \overline{37}\ \overline{6}\ \overline{28}\ \overline{31}$

F. 1600 Pennsylvania Avenue dwelling (2 wds.)

$\overline{27}\ \overline{26}\ \overline{81}\ \overline{61}\ \overline{38}\ \overline{46}\ \overline{20}\ \overline{33}\ \overline{75}\ \overline{56}$

G. Kings, queens, princes, princesses, etc.

$\overline{35}\ \overline{16}\ \overline{14}\ \overline{79}\ \overline{51}\ \overline{45}\ \overline{78}$

H. Without distinctive or stimulating qualities

$\overline{68}\ \overline{12}\ \overline{50}\ \overline{52}\ \overline{57}\ \overline{36}\ \overline{21}$

I. Sudden, sharp pains

$\overline{9}\ \overline{34}\ \overline{1}\ \overline{11}\ \overline{74}\ \overline{47}\ \overline{82}$

J. Focused on the task at hand

$\overline{66}\ \overline{8}\ \overline{54}\ \overline{49}\ \overline{43}\ \overline{30}$

K. Big rival of Adidas and New Balance shoes

$\overline{69}\ \overline{24}\ \overline{44}\ \overline{77}$

L. Mariah Carey's 2001 movie bomb

$\overline{70}\ \overline{76}\ \overline{62}\ \overline{25}\ \overline{40}\ \overline{18}\ \overline{48}$

Quotation Puzzle 7

1G		2H	3P	4N		5L	6I	7D	8A	9J		10M	11O	12H	13G		14F
	15B	16C	17L	18Q	19O	20D	21N	22M	23F	24H	25P	26A	27I		28L	29D	30M
31O	32A	33H		34N	35I	36D	37C		38I		39F	40I	41K	42L	43N	44H	
45C	46P		47Q	48M	49B		50P	51A	52B	53D		54H	55M	56N		57O	58M
59F	60H		61P	62L	63Q	64G	65M		66F	67E	68P		69H	70L	71Q	72K	73C
74P		75L	76F	77D	78H		79M	80I		81N	82J	83M		84G	85F	86K	
87G	88Q	89J	90H	91A	92K	93M	94L	95C	96E	97I	98O		99E	100B	101Q	102K	
103E	104J	105N	106L	107P		108K	109N	110H		111A	112D	113I	114K	115F	116O		117N
118B	119E	120P	121K	122A	123F	124J											

Clues:

A. Moviedom's Scorpion King (2 wds.)

$\overline{26}\ \overline{91}\ \overline{111}\ \overline{122}\ \overline{51}\ \overline{32}\ \overline{8}$

B. Throaty voices or woodshop tools

$\overline{118}\ \overline{100}\ \overline{49}\ \overline{15}\ \overline{52}$

C. Atlanta hip-hop star of "Nice & Slow"

$\overline{45}\ \overline{16}\ \overline{37}\ \overline{73}\ \overline{95}$

D. French privateer who aided the U.S. Revolutionary War

$\overline{7}\ \overline{112}\ \overline{29}\ \overline{20}\ \overline{36}\ \overline{77}\ \overline{53}$

E. Super Mario Bros. star who has his own island

$\overline{103}\ \overline{119}\ \overline{99}\ \overline{67}\ \overline{96}$

F. Maze of intricate paths

$\overline{123}\ \overline{14}\ \overline{39}\ \overline{59}\ \overline{23}\ \overline{76}\ \overline{115}\ \overline{66}\ \overline{85}$

G. Likely (2 wds.)

$\overline{1}\ \overline{87}\ \overline{64}\ \overline{84}\ \overline{13}$

H. Branch of numbers dealing with relationships and proportions

$\overline{2}\ \overline{44}\ \overline{12}\ \overline{78}\ \overline{33}\ \overline{69}\ \overline{54}\ \overline{110}\ \overline{24}\ \overline{90}\ \overline{60}$

I. China, Japan, Korea, etc., collectively (2 wds.)

$\overline{80}\ \overline{6}\ \overline{27}\ \overline{113}\ \overline{40}\ \overline{97}\ \overline{35}\ \overline{38}$

J. Toys you might "walk the dog" with (hyph.)

$\overline{124}\ \overline{82}\ \overline{89}\ \overline{104}\ \overline{9}$

K. Theory of relativity promulgator

$\overline{121}\ \overline{114}\ \overline{41}\ \overline{102}\ \overline{72}\ \overline{86}\ \overline{92}\ \overline{108}$

L. Get rid of some trash (2 wds.)

$\overline{94}\ \overline{62}\ \overline{106}\ \overline{28}\ \overline{75}\ \overline{42}\ \overline{5}\ \overline{70}\ \overline{17}$

M. Extreme, uncritical zealousness for a cause

$\overline{30}\ \overline{58}\ \overline{55}\ \overline{93}\ \overline{22}\ \overline{10}\ \overline{83}\ \overline{48}\ \overline{65}\ \overline{79}$

N. Reversing direction, like Answer J? (hyph.)

$\overline{105}\ \overline{117}\ \overline{21}\ \overline{4}\ \overline{56}\ \overline{81}\ \overline{109}\ \overline{34}\ \overline{43}$

O. Parts of the day following sunset

$\overline{11}\ \overline{31}\ \overline{116}\ \overline{19}\ \overline{98}\ \overline{57}$

P. Periodical delivered daily to your door

$\overline{50}\ \overline{68}\ \overline{61}\ \overline{25}\ \overline{46}\ \overline{3}\ \overline{120}\ \overline{107}\ \overline{74}$

Q. Seagoing crafts for the wealthy

$\overline{101}\ \overline{63}\ \overline{18}\ \overline{47}\ \overline{71}\ \overline{88}$

Quotation Puzzle 8

1F	2C	■	3G	4R	5J	6K	■	7E	8H	9O	10G	■	11B	12L	13F	14G
■	15S	16N	■	17A	■	18R	19C	20P	21K	22Q	23L	24M	25A	26S	■	27M	28Q
29P	30K	31I	■	32B	33F	■	34M	35Q	36J	■	37E	38R	39J	40O	41C	■	42E
43A	44R	45S	46C	■	47H	48A	49G	50L	■	51B	52Q	53G	54L	55D	■	56J	57F
■	58F	59H	60N	61E	■	62L	63K	64D	■	65L	66H	67O	68F	69R	70A	71E	72S
■	73N	74S	■	75A	76F	77L	78O	79P	■	80N	81A	82G	■	83R	84D	85L	■
86L	87A	88D	89F	■	90M	91K	92H	93R	94N	95A	■	96J	97C	■	98I	99P	100F
101R	102B	■	103L	104I	■	105A	106B	107F	■	108I	109M	■	110A	■	111B	112I	113M

Clues:

A. Diva of the No. 1 hits "Heartbreaker" and "Honey" (2 wds.)

$\overline{70}$ $\overline{87}$ $\overline{43}$ $\overline{110}$ $\overline{17}$ $\overline{48}$ $\overline{25}$ $\overline{81}$ $\overline{95}$ $\overline{75}$ $\overline{105}$

B. Inuit houses made of ice

$\overline{32}$ $\overline{51}$ $\overline{11}$ $\overline{111}$ $\overline{106}$ $\overline{102}$

C. Food Channel stars such as Emeril Lagasse

$\overline{41}$ $\overline{46}$ $\overline{19}$ $\overline{97}$ $\overline{2}$

D. Borders of garments such as dresses

$\overline{84}$ $\overline{64}$ $\overline{88}$ $\overline{55}$

E. Reduce in amount, degree, or intensity

$\overline{7}$ $\overline{37}$ $\overline{71}$ $\overline{42}$ $\overline{61}$

F. Comprehensive; thorough

$\overline{57}$ $\overline{76}$ $\overline{58}$ $\overline{1}$ $\overline{107}$ $\overline{33}$ $\overline{100}$ $\overline{68}$ $\overline{13}$ $\overline{89}$

G. These fall off trees

$\overline{3}$ $\overline{10}$ $\overline{49}$ $\overline{53}$ $\overline{14}$ $\overline{82}$

H. Close cousins of butterflies

$\overline{92}$ $\overline{59}$ $\overline{47}$ $\overline{66}$ $\overline{8}$

I. Places where you'd cook pizza

$\overline{108}$ $\overline{98}$ $\overline{31}$ $\overline{112}$ $\overline{104}$

J. Signs or portents of good or evil

$\overline{96}$ $\overline{56}$ $\overline{36}$ $\overline{5}$ $\overline{39}$

K. The ____ Riders (Teddy Roosevelt's outfit)

$\overline{30}$ $\overline{21}$ $\overline{91}$ $\overline{6}$ $\overline{63}$

L. Gets out of tough spots or predicaments

$\overline{85}$ $\overline{77}$ $\overline{62}$ $\overline{23}$ $\overline{12}$ $\overline{65}$ $\overline{103}$ $\overline{50}$ $\overline{54}$ $\overline{86}$

M. Excessively or showily decorated

$\overline{34}$ $\overline{109}$ $\overline{90}$ $\overline{24}$ $\overline{27}$ $\overline{113}$

N. Make a call

$\overline{60}$ $\overline{80}$ $\overline{73}$ $\overline{16}$ $\overline{94}$

O. Des Moines's state

$\overline{40}$ $\overline{78}$ $\overline{9}$ $\overline{67}$

P. "Finding ____" (animated underwater movie)

$\overline{79}$ $\overline{29}$ $\overline{20}$ $\overline{99}$

Q. 1/12 of a foot

$\overline{52}$ $\overline{35}$ $\overline{22}$ $\overline{28}$

R. Unmoved by pity or tenderness; stubborn

$\overline{4}$ $\overline{93}$ $\overline{18}$ $\overline{44}$ $\overline{69}$ $\overline{38}$ $\overline{83}$ $\overline{101}$

S. Very good, fine, excellent

$\overline{72}$ $\overline{15}$ $\overline{74}$ $\overline{45}$ $\overline{26}$

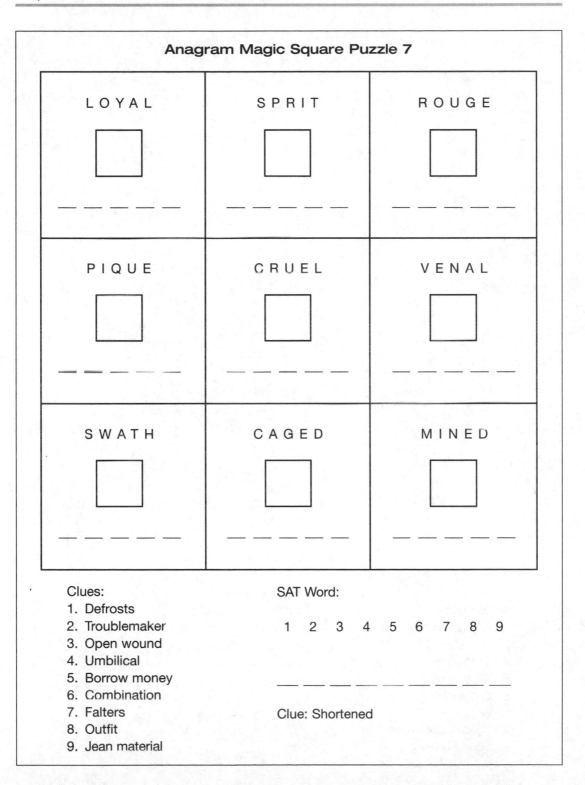

Anagram Magic Square Puzzle 7

LOYAL

SPRIT

ROUGE

PIQUE

CRUEL

VENAL

SWATH

CAGED

MINED

Clues:
1. Defrosts
2. Troublemaker
3. Open wound
4. Umbilical
5. Borrow money
6. Combination
7. Falters
8. Outfit
9. Jean material

SAT Word:

1   2   3   4   5   6   7   8   9

＿ ＿ ＿ ＿ ＿ ＿ ＿ ＿ ＿

Clue: Shortened

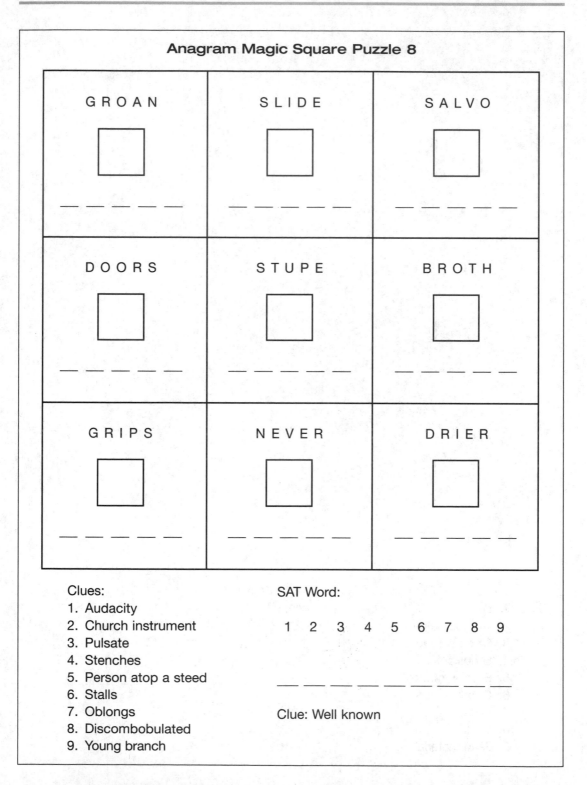

Anagram Magic Square Puzzle 8

GROAN

SLIDE

SALVO

DOORS

STUPE

BROTH

GRIPS

NEVER

DRIER

Clues:
1. Audacity
2. Church instrument
3. Pulsate
4. Stenches
5. Person atop a steed
6. Stalls
7. Oblongs
8. Discombobulated
9. Young branch

SAT Word:

1   2   3   4   5   6   7   8   9

— — — — — — — — —

Clue: Well known

Anagram Magic Square Puzzle 9

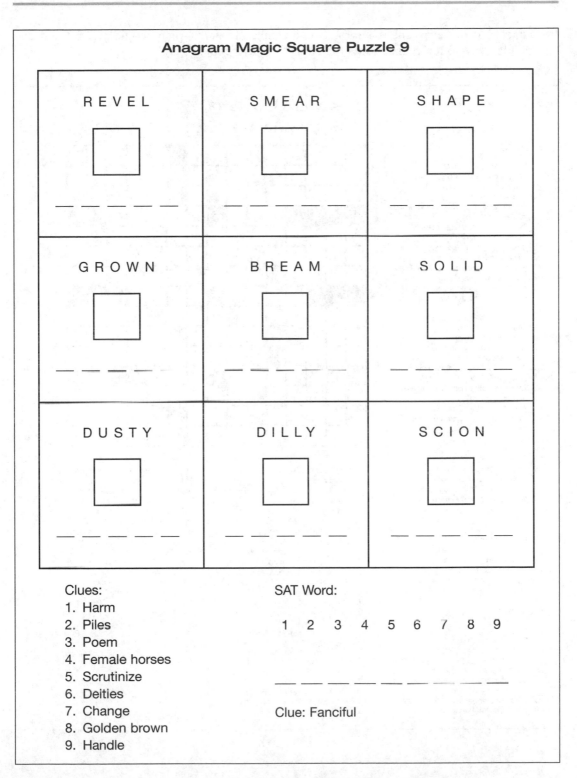

REVEL

SMEAR

SHAPE

GROWN

BREAM

SOLID

DUSTY

DILLY

SCION

Clues:
1. Harm
2. Piles
3. Poem
4. Female horses
5. Scrutinize
6. Deities
7. Change
8. Golden brown
9. Handle

SAT Word:

1 2 3 4 5 6 7 8 9

Clue: Fanciful

It's a fact that not everyone is honest. Some people are liars; some people are out and out cheats. Here are some special words for these "Sneaky people."

Crossword Puzzle 13
Sneaky People

ACROSS

1. Lights that sit on tables
6. Streets or roads (abbr.)
9. Make or become confused
14. Expect; look for
15. French word for "water" (homonym of "oh")
16. Test answers that aren't falses
17. Misleading; fraudulent
19. Inner _____ (river float trip "vehicles")
20. Tell a falsehood
21. Mushrooms and molds, collectively
23. Treacherous; perfidious
28. Spiritual part of a human being
31. Ovens for firing pottery
32. Mistake; goof
34. Frequent American stadium chant
35. Leave off intentionally
36. Chair or table "prop"
37. Handbags or pocketbooks
39. Peruse a book
41. Society for treating animals well (anagram of "tape")
42. Extremely bad reputation because of an outrage
45. Founding Father Franklin
46. Born and _____ (grew up there)
50. "Brains" of a PC (abbr.)
51. "Desperately Seeking _____" (Madonna movie)
53. Dwelling; place of residence
54. Makes a mistake
56. Ruinous; injurious; hurtful
58. City in Oklahoma (anagram of "salut")
60. Six-legged picnic intruder
61. Spanish word for "friend"
63. Cooperating secretly; conspiring
69. Exploding stars
70. Diner table scrap (anagram of "rot")
71. Leonardo da _____ (Italian artist)
72. Bambi and all his kind
73. "Scream" movie director Craven
74. _____ a positive note (conclude happily) (2 wds.)

DOWN

1. Young boy
2. Overwhelm with fear
3. Apple PC, for short
4. "American _____" (Jason Biggs comedy)
5. "Tall" circus performers walk on these
6. Officiated at a basketball game
7. Greek letter for "tee"
8. Brimstone or matchhead element
9. Envelope notation (abbr.)
10. Substances used to treat illness
11. Questionable or doubtful
12. Actors Horsley or Majors (anagram of "eel")
13. Letter before "tee"
18. Spanish word for "uncle"
22. Annual American tennis championship (2 wds.)
23. Boxing technical win, for short
24. Metal part of a basketball hoop
25. Heavyweight boxing champ "The Greatest"
26. Prefix meaning "within"
27. Relative of .com
29. Put to work; employ
30. _____ Vegas, Nevada
33. In a _____ (bored and stale)
36. Easy basketball scores
38. Chief religious figure at a synagogue
40. Letters before "en"
41. Long, tapering flags
42. Frozen water
43. National Public Radio (abbr.)
44. Done surreptitiously or by stealth
45. Unit of soap or candy
47. Tigger's friend and Kanga's son
48. School relative of .com
49. _____ Moines, Iowa (city)
52. Manatee or dugong (2 wds.)
53. On the move and doing things
55. Cereal or tea sweetener
57. Ramada _____ (motel chain)
59. Not a win
61. As well as
62. Curly, _____, and Larry (The Three Stooges)
64. Mineral-bearing rock
65. Action movie star Diesel
66. State due west of Ohio (abbr.)
67. Sergeant or corporal (abbr.) (anagram of "con")
68. Cotton _____ (machine for separating out cotton seeds)

Some people seem to have all the luck; they have everything they want and more. Sometimes all we can say to them is: "Too much, man."

Crossword Puzzle 14
Too Much, Man

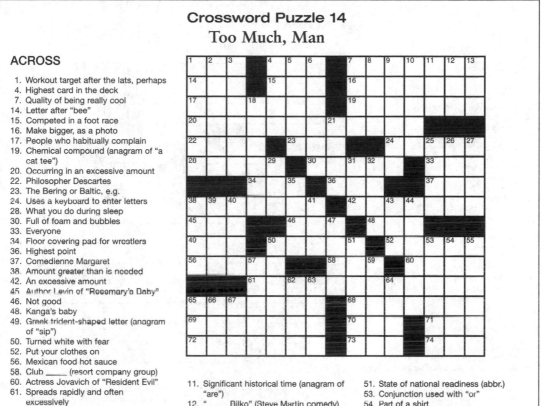

ACROSS

1. Workout target after the lats, perhaps
4. Highest card in the deck
7. Quality of being really cool
14. Letter after "bee"
15. Competed in a foot race
16. Make bigger, as a photo
17. People who habitually complain
19. Chemical compound (anagram of "a cat tee")
20. Occurring in an excessive amount
22. Philosopher Descartes
23. The Bering or Baltic, e.g.
24. Uses a keyboard to enter letters
28. What you do during sleep
30. Full of foam and bubbles
33. Everyone
34. Floor covering pad for wrestlers
36. Highest point
37. Comedienne Margaret
38. Amount greater than is needed
42. An excessive amount
45. Author Levin of "Rosemary's Baby"
46. Not good
48. Kanga's baby
49. Greek trident-shaped letter (anagram of "sip")
50. Turned white with fear
52. Put your clothes on
56. Mexican food hot sauce
58. Club _____ (resort company group)
60. Actress Jovavich of "Resident Evil"
61. Spreads rapidly and often excessively
65. Deprive and make desolate
68. Items you wear
69. "Slots spots" for gamester teens
70. Cheerios cereal grain
71. Adam's Garden of Eden wife
72. People ripping things up
73. The Big Apple's initials
74. Seeing ___ (extremely angry)

DOWN

1. Be in agreement or harmony
2. Mammal that builds its own dam
3. Calm, quiet, and peaceful
4. Length times width product
5. What runners load up on before a marathon
6. Follows in order
7. This rests on your shoulders
8. Native Peruvian of the Andes
9. Full or abundant supply
10. Sharply or smartly dressed
11. Significant historical time (anagram of "are")
12. "_____ Bilko" (Steve Martin comedy) (abbr.)
13. Use your eyes
18. Sound booster part of a stereo (anagram of "pamper")
21. Suffix with "astro" or "cosmo"
25. Set the _____ (lead the race)
26. Kindergarten to senior year catchall (abbr.)
27. Soda machine coin receptacle
29. Prefix meaning "bad" or "ill"
31. MS-_____ (PC operating system)
32. Metal attachment to a cowboy boot
35. Biggest brass instrument in the marching band
38. Short, quick drinks
39. _____ Major (the Big Dipper)
40. Part of a train track
41. "My Gal _____" (Erie Canal song)
43. Fishing pole, e.g.
44. Prepare a diskette for use on your PC
47. Actress Moore of "GI Jane"
50. Thanksgiving or St. Patrick's Day event
51. State of national readiness (abbr.)
53. Conjunction used with "or"
54. Part of a shirt
55. Talked back or acted up
57. Arm a castle tower guard might carry
59. Put off to a later time
62. _____ and above
63. Not more
64. Campus military organization (abbr.)
65. Baseball hitter's need
66. "Able was I _____ I saw Elba"
67. Electronics company with a dog logo

We all feel sad at one time or another. Things we can't control sometimes overwhelm us. Here are some words for when you're feeling particularly low or "Bummed out."

Crossword Puzzle 15
Bummed Out

ACROSS

1. _____ in the mouth (bummed out)
5. Brothers famous for fairy tales
10. A real _____ (definitely a bummer)
14. Entertainers Clapton or Idle
15. Big craze
16. The Hawkeye State
17. Gloomy and maybe even depressed
19. Dog-powered Eskimo vehicle
20. Greek letters meaning very small amounts
21. Actor Stephen of "The Crying Game" (anagram of "are")
22. "Clean up this _____" (Mom's orders when seeing your room)
23. Got on in years
26. Railroad stop (abbr.)
28. Possess
32. "Signatures" from those who can't write
34. Mary-Kate and Ashley's last name
38. Teheran's country
39. Tax put on imported goods
41. Heavyweight champ played by Will Smith
42. Bummed out and sorrowful
44. Foolishly sentimental
46. String bean comic Philips
47. Joins an online users list (2 wds.)
49. On the ocean (hopefully in a boat!)
50. Language of modern Teheran (anagram of "fairs")
52. Bird of "The Ugly Duckling" tale
53. Catholic church service
54. Getting along in years
56. "Dragonwyck" novelist Seton
58. MTV's "The _____ World"
61. Relative of .com or .gov
63. Suggest without stating explicitly
68. Impel with force or words
69. Unrelievedly mournful or gloomy
72. Bummed out or dejected
73. Seriously overweight
74. What many people's hair does
75. Spotted with one's eyes
76. Aired a TV show a second time
77. Greek god of war

DOWN

1. Actress Moore of "GI Jane"
2. Cream-filled black cookie
3. Shrink from the heat, like lettuce
4. College sports ruling body (abbr.)
5. Auto maker of Suburbans and Yukons (abbr.)
6. Cheerleader's word
7. Lined up alphabetically or numerically (2 wds.)
8. 5280 feet, e.g.
9. Ancient natives of Mexico's Yucatan
10. Bad enough to bum you out
11. Actor's part
12. Overwhelms with fear
13. Wanders about restlessly from place to place
18. U.S. intelligence gathering outfit (acronym)
24. Start the day off (2 wds.)
25. Praises or extols
27. Food also called bean curd
28. Super quality television signal (abbr.)
29. Good or enticing smell
30. Bravery in the face of danger
31. Chemical suffix used after benz or ethyl
33. Characteristic of apes or monkeys
35. Mexican food hot sauce
36. Writer Wiesel and designer Tahari (anagram of "Elsie")
37. Spanish word for "girls"
40. Actress Brice or Ardant (or what you sit on!)
43. Aluminum or tin _____ (kitchen wrap)
45. River-blocking construction of a beaver
48. Strut about boastfully
51. Grave, sober, or mirthless
55. Sorrow or grief (anagram of "drool")
57. What we breathe
58. Floor coverings or jokey words for toupees
59. Mystery writer _____ Stanley Gardner (anagram of "leer")
60. Catchall for fits, fevers, shivering, etc.
62. Easily bilked yokel or bumpkin (anagram of "uber")
64. Common, shiny, mountainside mineral
65. Put liquid into a glass
66. Entice; tempt
67. Logos seen on St. Laurent fashionwear
70. Popular chant at American sports events
71. Actor Affleck

Most people are good people: outgoing, warm and friendly. And there are lots of convivial words to describe them. Here are some nice words for some "Affable people."

Crossword Puzzle 16
Affable People

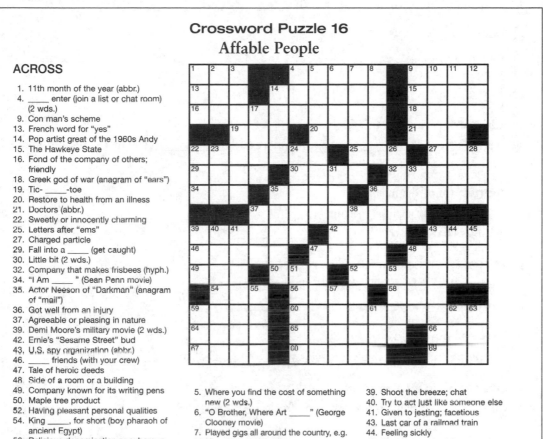

ACROSS

1. 11th month of the year (abbr.)
4. _____ enter (join a list or chat room) (2 wds.)
9. Con man's scheme
13. French word for "yes"
14. Pop artist great of the 1960s Andy
15. The Hawkeye State
16. Fond of the company of others; friendly
18. Greek god of war (anagram of "ears")
19. Tic- _____-toe
20. Restore to health from an illness
21. Doctors (abbr.)
22. Sweetly or innocently charming
25. Letters after "ems"
27. Charged particle
29. Fall into a _____ (get caught)
30. Little bit (2 wds.)
32. Company that makes frisbees (hyph.)
34. "I Am _____ " (Sean Penn movie)
35. Actor Neeson of "Darkman" (anagram of "mail")
36. Got well from an injury
37. Agreeable or pleasing in nature
39. Demi Moore's military movie (2 wds.)
42. Ernie's "Sesame Street" bud
43. U.S. spy organization (abbr.)
46. _____ friends (with your crew)
47. Tale of heroic deeds
48. Side of a room or a building
49. Company known for its writing pens
50. Maple tree product
52. Having pleasant personal qualities
54. King _____, for short (boy pharaoh of ancient Egypt)
56. Religious denomination or subgroup
58. _____ de Janeiro, Brazil
59. Country in western Africa
60. Well suited for the occasion; apt
64. Latin abbrievation for "and others" (2 wds.)
65. Hateful; detestable
66. Health or fitness club
67. Actor Richard of "Pretty Woman"
68. ABC televison innovator Arledge (anagram of "one or")
69. Prefix meaning "environment"

DOWN

1. Egg _____ (holiday drink)
2. "_____ Town" (Thornton Wilder play)
3. Hanoi and Saigon's country
4. What you row with
5. Where you find the cost of something new (2 wds.)
6. "O Brother, Where Art _____" (George Clooney movie)
7. Played gigs all around the country, e.g.
8. Mary-Kate and Ashley _____
9. "Anna and the King of _____"
10. Gracious; friendly; warm
11. "Totally spectacular, dude!"
12. Mothers, for short
14. Texas city on the Brazos River
17. Sudden breath from surprise or shock
22. Pounds, ounces, etc. (abbr.)
23. Author Levin of "Rosemary's Baby"
24. Northeasternmost American state
26. Perspiration
28. Say yes nonverbally
31. Single-celled organism
33. Mark Twain portrayer Holbrook
35. Yearns for; pines
36. Biblical king of Tyre (anagram of "I harm")
37. Soup or tuna fish container
38. The act of denying
39. Shoot the breeze; chat
40. Try to act just like someone else
41. Given to jesting; facetious
43. Last car of a railroad train
44. Feeling sickly
45. Ginger _____ (soda)
47. Company known for its swimsuits
48. Bide one's time
51. "_____ me, I'll pass" (2 wds.)
53. Opening where light enters the pupil of the eye
55. Scrabble game piece
57. Award given to TV commercials (anagram of "coil")
59. Actress Ryan of "When Harry Met Sally"
61. Actor's prompt
62. What bar code scanners scan (abbr.)
63. _____ Paulo, Brazil

Hidden Meanings Puzzle 9

in·tran·si·gent (in tran´si jənt), *adj.*
1. refusing to agree or _____(10); _____(14); _____(10).

co·gent (kō´jənt), *adj.*
1. convincing or _____(10) by virtue of _____(8), clear, or _____(8) presentation; telling.
2. to the point; _____(8); _____(9).

re·dun·dant (ri dun´dənt), *adj.*
1. characterized by _____(9) or unnecessary _____(10) in expressing ideas; _____(6).

hum·drum (hum´drum´), *adj.*
1. _____(7) variety; boring; _____(4).
2. tedious character or _____(7); _____(8).

prod·i·gal (prod´i gəl), *adj.*
1. wastefully or _____(10) _____(11).
2. giving or yielding _____(9); _____(6).

im·pu·dent (im´pyə dənt), *adj.*
1. of, pertaining to, or characterized by _____(12) or _____(10).

lo·qua·cious (lō kwā´shəs), *adj.*
1. talking or tending to talk much or freely; _____(9); _____(10); babbling; _____(9).
2. characterized by _____(9) talk; _____(5).

con·sen·sus (kən sen´səs), *n., pl.* **-sus·es.**
1. _____(8) of _____(7).
2. general agreement or _____(7); _____(7).

ig·no·min·y (ig´nə min´ē, ig nom´ə nē), *n., pl.* **-min·ies.**
1. _____(8); dishonor; public _____(8).
2. _____(8) or dishonorable quality or _____(7) or an instance of this.

ma·lign (mə līn´), *v.t.*
1. to speak _____(7) untruths about; speak _____(4) of; _____(7); _____(6).
2. evil in effect; _____(10); baleful; _____(9).

Hidden Meanings Puzzle 9 *(continued)*

4 LETTERS	*8 LETTERS*	10 LETTERS
EVIL	DISGRACE	CHATTERING
DULL	MONOTONY	EFFRONTERY
	INCISIVE	BELIEVABLE
5 LETTERS	SHAMEFUL	PERNICIOUS
WORDY	MAJORITY	RECKLESSLY
	CONTEMPT	INFLEXIBLE
6 LETTERS	FORCEFUL	COMPROMISE
LAVISH	RELEVANT	REPETITION
PROLIX		
DEFAME	*9 LETTERS*	*11 LETTERS*
	PERTINENT	EXTRAVAGANT
7 LETTERS	PROFUSELY	
ROUTINE	EXCESSIVE	*12 LETTERS*
CONCORD	TALKATIVE	IMPERTINENCE
SLANDER	VERBOSITY	
LACKING	GARRULOUS	*14 LETTERS*
HARMONY	INJURIOUS	UNCOMPROMISING
HARMFUL		
OPINION		
CONDUCT		

Some words in a particular definition will be interchangeable.

Hidden Meanings Puzzle 10

ab·er·ra·tion (ab´ə ra´shən), *n.*

1. the act of departing from the _____(5), normal, or usual _____(6).
2. the act of _____(9) from the _____(8), usual, or normal type.

in·sid·i·ous (in sid´ē əs), *adj.*

1. intended to _____(6) or _____(7).
2. stealthily _____(11) or deceitful.
3. operating or proceeding in an _____(13) or seemingly harmless way but actually with _____(5) effect.

jux·ta·pose (juk´stə pōz´, juk´stə pōz´), *v.t.,* **-posed, -pos·ing.**

1. to place close _____(8) or side by side, especially for _____(10) or _____(8).

joc·u·lar (jok´yə lər), *adj.*

1. given to, characterized by, intended for, or suited to joking or _____(7); waggish; _____(9).

in·ter·mi·na·ble (in tûr´mə nə bəl), *adj.*

1. incapable of being _____(10); _____(8).
2. _____(12) or annoyingly _____(10) or continued; unceasing; _____(9).

lag·gard (lag´ərd), *n.*

1. a person or thing that lags; _____(8); _____(8).
2. moving, developing, or responding slowly; _____(8); _____(8); backward.

prone (prōn), *adj.*

1. having a natural _____(11) or tendency to something; _____(8); _____(6).
2. having the front or _____(7) part downward; _____(5) face downward.

trite (trīt), *adj.,* **trit·er, trit·est.**

1. lacking in freshness or _____(13) because of constant use or _____(9) repetition; _____(9).

vo·li·tion (vō lish´ən, və-), *n.*

1. the act of willing, choosing, or _____(9).
2. a choice or _____(8) made by the will.

un·ten·a·ble (un ten´ə bəl), *adj.*

1. _____(9) of being _____(8), as an argument, thesis, and so on; _____(12).
2. not fit to be _____(8), as an apartment, house, and the like.

Hidden Meanings Puzzle 10 (continued)

5 LETTERS
GRAVE
LYING
RIGHT

6 LETTERS
LIABLE
ENTRAP
COURSE

7 LETTERS
JESTING
BEGUILE
VENTRAL

8 LETTERS
DISPOSED
TOGETHER
LOITERER
ORDINARY
UNENDING
DILATORY
DECISION
OCCUPIED
LINGERER
DEFENDED
CONTRAST
SLUGGISH

9 LETTERS
INCESSANT
RESOLVING
EXCESSIVE
DEVIATING
FACETIOUS
HACKNEYED
INCAPABLE

10 LETTERS
COMPARISON
PROTRACTED
TERMINATED

11 LETTERS
TREACHEROUS
INCLINATION

12 LETTERS
INDEFENSIBLE
MONOTONOUSLY

13 LETTERS
EFFECTIVENESS
INCONSPICUOUS

Some words in a particular definition will be interchangeable.

Hidden Meanings Puzzle 11

a·mal·ga·mate (ə malʹgə māt´), *v.,* **-mat·ed, -mat·ing.** —*v.t.*

1. to mix or _____(5) so as to make a _____(11); blend; unite; combine.
2. to combine, unite, merge, or _____(8).

clois·tered (kloiʹstərd), *adj.*

1. _____(8) from the world; _____(9).

tal·is·man (talʹis mən, -iz-), *n., pl.* **-mans.**

1. a stone, _____(4), or other object, _____(8) with figures or _____(10) supposed to possess _____(6) powers and worn as an _____(6) or charm.

in·an·i·mate (in anʹə mit), *adj.*

1. not animate; _____(8).
2. spiritless; _____(8); _____(4).

per·plex·i·ty (pər plekʹsi tē), *n., pl.* **-ities.**

1. the state of being perplexed; _____(9); _____(11).
2. a _____(7), involved, or confused condition or _____(9).

e·nig·ma (ə nigʹmə), *n., pl.* **-mas, -ma·ta** (-mə tə).

1. a puzzling or _____(12) occurrence or situation.
2. a person of puzzling or _____(13) character.
3. a saying, question, picture, and the like, containing a _____(6) meaning; _____(6).

crass (kras), *adj.,* **-er, -est.**

1. without _____(10), delicacy, or _____(11); gross; _____(6); stupid.

for·tu·i·tous (fôr tooʹtəs, -tyoo´-), *adj.*

1. _____(9) or produced by _____(6); _____(10).
2. _____(5); _____(9).

pre·pos·ter·ous (pri posʹtər əs, -trəs), *adj.*

1. completely _____(8) to nature, _____(6), or common sense; _____(6); senseless; utterly _____(7).

squal·id (skwolʹid, skwôʹlid), *adj.*

1. foul and _____(9), as from lack of care or cleanliness; _____(9) and _____(6).
2. wretched; miserable; _____(8); _____(6).

Hidden Meanings Puzzle 11 *(continued)*

4 LETTERS
DULL
RING

5 LETTERS
LUCKY
MERGE

6 LETTERS
AMULET
FILTHY
HIDDEN
CHANCE
OCCULT
ABSURD
SORDID
OBTUSE
RIDDLE
REASON

7 LETTERS
FOOLISH
TANGLED

8 LETTERS
SECLUDED
CONTRARY
SLUGGISH
DEGRADED
LIFELESS
COALESCE
ENGRAVED

9 LETTERS
HAPPENING
REPULSIVE
SHELTERED
SITUATION
FORTUNATE
CONFUSION
NEGLECTED

10 LETTERS
REFINEMENT
ACCIDENTAL
CHARACTERS

11 LETTERS
UNCERTAINTY
SENSITIVITY
COMBINATION

12 LETTERS
INEXPLICABLE

13 LETTERS
CONTRADICTORY

Some words in a particular definition will be interchangeable.

Hidden Meanings Puzzle 12

up·roar·i·ous (up rôr´ē əs, -rōr´-), *adj.*

1. characterized by or in a state of uproar; _____(10).

2. making an uproar; _____(8) and _____(5), as an assembly, person, and so on.

win·some (win´səm), *adj.*

1. sweetly or _____(10) charming; _____(7); _____(8).

plun·der (plun´dər), *v.t.*

1. to rob of goods or _____(9) by open _____(5), as in war, _____(7) raids, _____(10), and so forth.

2. to rob, despoil, or _____(6).

3. to take wrongfully, as by _____(7), robbery, or _____(5).

har·row·ing (har´ō ing), *adj.*

1. extremely _____(10) or distressing; _____(8).

gar·gan·tu·an (gär gan´choo ən), *adj.*

1. _____(8); _____(8); _____(8).

churl·ish (chûr´lish), *adj.*

1. like a churl; _____(7); rude.

2. of a churl; _____(11).

whee·dle (hwēd´l, wēd´l), *v.*, **-dled, -dling.** —*v.t.*

1. to _____(8) to influence (a person) by smooth, _____(10), or _____(9) words or acts.

fal·la·cious (fə lā´shəs), *adj.*

1. containing a _____(7); logically _____(7).

2. _____(9); misleading.

con·geal (kən jēl´), *v.t., v.i.*

1. to change from a soft or _____(5) state to a _____(5) or solid state, as by cooling or _____(8).

2. to curdle; _____(9), as a fluid.

fi·as·co (fē as´kō *or, esp. for 2,* -ä´skō), *n., pl.* **-cos, -coes.**

1. a complete and _____(11) _____(7).

Hidden Meanings Puzzle 12 *(continued)*

5 LETTERS	7 LETTERS	9 LETTERS
FRAUD	BOORISH	VALUABLES
FLUID	WINNING	COAGULATE
FORCE	HOSTILE	BEGUILING
RIGID	UNSOUND	DECEPTIVE
NOISY	FAILURE	
	FALLACY	10 LETTERS
6 LETTERS	PILLAGE	FLATTERING
FLEECE		DISTURBING
	8 LETTERS	TUMULTUOUS
	GIGANTIC	INNOCENTLY
	ENGAGING	BRIGANDAGE
	FREEZING	
	COLOSSAL	11 LETTERS
	ENDEAVOR	IGNOMINIOUS
	GRIEVOUS	PEASANTLIKE
	ENORMOUS	
	CONFUSED	

Some words in a particular definition will be interchangeable.

Hidden Meanings Puzzle 13

wraith (rāth), *n.*

1. an _____(10) of a living person supposed to _____(7) his or her death.
2. a _____(7) _____(6).

pro·pin·qui·ty (prō ping′kwi tē), *n.*

1. nearness in place; _____(9).
2. nearness of relation; _____(7).
3. _____(8) of nature; _____(10).

ep·i·taph (ep′i taf′, -täf′), *n.*

1. a commemorative _____(11) on a _____(4) or _____(8) monument about the person buried at that site.
2. a brief _____(4) or other writing in praise of a _____(8) person.

a·byss (ə bis′), *n.*

1. a deep, _____(12) space, gulf, or _____(6); _____(4) chasm.
2. anything _____(8), _____(12), or _____(8).

par·a·gon (par′ə gon′, -gən), *n.*

1. a model or _____(7) of _____(10) or of a _____(10) excellence.

vis·cer·al (vis′ər əl), *adj.*

1. of or pertaining to the _____(7).
2. characterized by or proceeding from _____(8) rather than _____(9).
3. characterized by or dealing with _____(6) or base emotions; _____(6).

per·spi·cac·i·ty (pûr′spi kas′i tē), *n.*

1. _____(8) of mental _____(10) and understanding; _____(11); _____(11).

de·ci·pher (di sī′fər), *v.t.*

1. to make out the _____(7) of [poor or partially _____(11) writing, etc.]
2. to discover the meaning of [anything _____(7) or difficult to _____(5) or _____(10)].

fa·cade (fə säd′, fa-), *n.*

1. *Architecture:* the _____(5) of a building, especially an _____(8) or _____(10) one.
2. a _____(11) appearance or _____(8) of something.

pru·ri·ent (prŏŏr′ē ənt), *adj.*

1. having, inclined to have, or characterized by _____(10) or _____(7) thoughts, _____(7), and the like.

Hidden Meanings Puzzle 13 *(continued)*

4 LETTERS
VAST
POEM
TOMB

5 LETTERS
TRACE
FRONT

6 LETTERS
CAVITY
EARTHY
SPIRIT
COARSE

7 LETTERS
MEANING
VISIBLE
PATTERN
VISCERA
KINSHIP
PORTEND
OBSCURE
DESIRES
LUSTFUL

8 LETTERS
ILLUSION
AFFINITY
MORTUARY
INSTINCT
PROFOUND
DECEASED
KEENNESS
INFINITE
IMPOSING

9 LETTERS
INTELLECT
PROXIMITY

10 LETTERS
PARTICULAR
DECORATIVE
LASCIVIOUS
SIMILARITY
EXCELLENCE
UNDERSTAND
PERCEPTION
APPARITION

11 LETTERS
OBLITERATED
INSCRIPTION
DISCERNMENT
SUPERFICIAL
PENETRATION

12 LETTERS
IMMEASURABLE
UNFATHOMABLE

Some words in a particular definition will be interchangeable.

END NOTE

You are making good progress! New words should be less intimidating and more interesting. Your vocabulary is growing, as is your ability to decode words. Watch for the new words you have learned in the books you read for school. The next chapter includes more difficult word connection puzzles. You are ready for them.

Fun Quiz

Which of the following would never be an SAT essay question/quotation?

1. It was the best of times, it was the worst of times. (Charles Dickens) Do you think the same could be said for our own times? Why or why not?

2. Should there be a law requiring U.S. citizens to marry only people of their own race?

3. The United States has declined to send its Olympic athletes to compete in the Olympic Games for political reasons. Should the Olympics be above politics, or are there circumstances where it is inappropriate for a country's athletes to compete in the Olympics?

4. Should the United States become a "neutral" country like Switzerland? Why or why not?

5. A man is known by the company his mind keeps. (Thomas Bailey Aldrich) Do you agree or disagree with Thomas Aldrich? Why?

Answer
Question 2 would never be on the SAT because the test is very politically correct, as it should be. Students of mixed race or those dating someone of another race could be upset by the question and score poorly on the SAT as a result. Also, a question that asks students to reveal their personal prejudices does not have a place on a standardized test.

In the critical reading section you may safely eliminate any answer choice that depicts an ethnic stereotype, denigrates any group, or makes fun of people for their religion.

There is considerable debate about the rewriting of the passages in the critical reading section. In order to not offend anyone taking the test, the test writers will rewrite a reading passage to eliminate any potentially offensive sections. Purists are appalled that great writers' work is being rewritten. They feel that students should be able to read the original work. Perhaps the SAT writers should ask the following essay question on the next SAT:

Should the SAT include texts in their original form even if they include potentially offensive material?

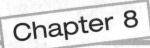

Chapter 8

CHALLENGING WORD CONNECTION PUZZLES

There are some words that will bring you up short, even drag you to a halt or make you quit. These are the words for when you've totally had it, when you're ready to say: "Enough already. I give up."

Crossword Puzzle 17
Enough Already. I Give Up.

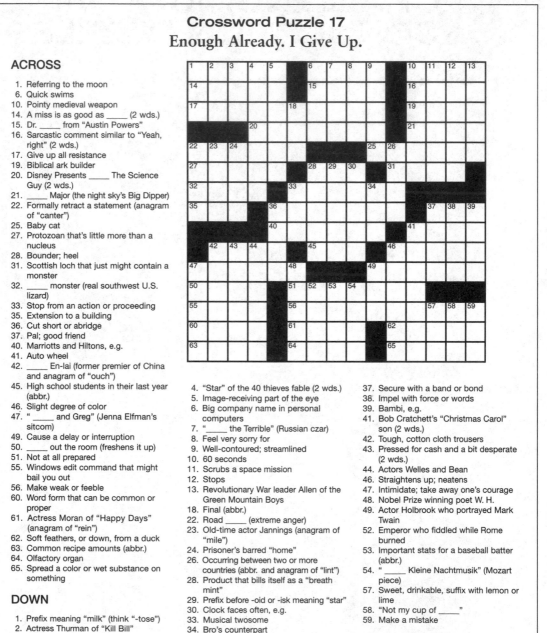

ACROSS

1. Referring to the moon
6. Quick swims
10. Pointy medieval weapon
14. A miss is as good as _____ (2 wds.)
15. Dr. _____ from "Austin Powers"
16. Sarcastic comment similar to "Yeah, right" (2 wds.)
17. Give up all resistance
19. Biblical ark builder
20. Disney Presents _____ The Science Guy (2 wds.)
21. _____ Major (the night sky's Big Dipper)
22. Formally retract a statement (anagram of "canter")
25. Baby cat
27. Protozoan that's little more than a nucleus
28. Bounder; heel
31. Scottish loch that just might contain a monster
32. _____ monster (real southwest U.S. lizard)
33. Stop from an action or proceeding
35. Extension to a building
36. Cut short or abridge
37. Pal; good friend
40. Marriotts and Hiltons, e.g.
41. Auto wheel
42. _____ En-lai (former premier of China and anagram of "ouch")
45. High school students in their last year (abbr.)
46. Slight degree of color
47. " _____ and Greg" (Jenna Elfman's sitcom)
49. Cause a delay or interruption
50. _____ out the room (freshens it up)
51. Not at all prepared
55. Windows edit command that might bail you out
56. Make weak or feeble
60. Word form that can be common or proper
61. Actress Moran of "Happy Days" (anagram of "rein")
62. Soft feathers, or down, from a duck
63. Common recipe amounts (abbr.)
64. Olfactory organ
65. Spread a color or wet substance on something

DOWN

1. Prefix meaning "milk" (think "-tose")
2. Actress Thurman of "Kill Bill"
3. Small bite
4. "Star" of the 40 thieves fable (2 wds.)
5. Image-receiving part of the eye
6. Big company name in personal computers
7. "_____ the Terrible" (Russian czar)
8. Feel very sorry for
9. Well-contoured; streamlined
10. 60 seconds
11. Scrubs a space mission
12. Stops
13. Revolutionary War leader Allen of the Green Mountain Boys
18. Final (abbr.)
22. Road _____ (extreme anger)
23. Old-time actor Jannings (anagram of "mile")
24. Prisoner's barred "home"
26. Occurring between two or more countries (abbr. and anagram of "lint")
28. Product that bills itself as a "breath mint"
29. Prefix before -oid or -isk meaning "star"
30. Clock faces often, e.g.
33. Musical twosome
34. Bro's counterpart
36. Pal; good friend
37. Secure with a band or bond
38. Impel with force or words
39. Bambi, e.g.
41. Bob Cratchett's "Christmas Carol" son (2 wds.)
42. Tough, cotton cloth trousers
43. Pressed for cash and a bit desperate (2 wds.)
44. Actors Welles and Bean
46. Straightens up; neatens
47. Intimidate; take away one's courage
48. Nobel Prize winning poet W. H.
49. Actor Holbrook who portrayed Mark Twain
52. Emperor who fiddled while Rome burned
53. Important stats for a baseball batter (abbr.)
54. " _____ Kleine Nachtmusik" (Mozart piece)
57. Sweet, drinkable, suffix with lemon or lime
58. "Not my cup of _____"
59. Make a mistake

Some people love to talk and talk and talk and talk. There are words for people who use a lot of words (or too many words)—people to whom we might wish to say, "Will you please be quiet!"

Crossword Puzzle 18
Will You Please Be Quiet!

ACROSS

1. Automobile
4. Fair hair color
10. _____ the Terrible (Russian czar)
14. How old you are
15. People using oars
16. Southwest table top land (anagram of "same")
17. Talking too much or too freely
19. Worship
20. Author Sinclair of "The Jungle"
21. Young woman coming out into society (for short)
22. Places where you live, dude
24. Excessively talkative; wordy
30. Without a stitch on
31. Test to see if clothes fit (2 wds.)
32. Workout or beauty spot
33. _____ Stadium (N.Y. Mets ballpark)
34. Marriotts or Hiltons, e.g.
35. Psychic's talent, for short
36. What Santa might bring you
38. Latin shorthand for "and so forth"
40. Actress Tyler of "Lord of the Rings"
43. Seaport and gulf in southwest Italy (anagram of "planes")
47. Overwhelms with fear
51. String bean comic Philips
52. _____ Mertz (Lucy Ricardo's best sitcom friend)
53. Get someone all worked up or angry
54. Inclined to gab a great deal
56. Aladdin found one in a bottle
57. Internet address hunting protocol (abbr.)
58. Very strong winds
60. Prefix meaning "both" and "around"
62. Crying out noisily; clamorous
67. On a _____ (has things going great)
68. Apprentice doctor or other professional
69. Frequent American arena chant
70. Central support structure of a ship (anagram of "leek")
71. Live and in _____ (appearing live)
72. Senator Kennedy of Mass., for short

DOWN

1. Record-setting Ripken of baseball
2. In time past
3. Need
4. Really rotten kids
5. Crazy (anagram of "cool")
6. Because of (2 wds.)
7. Prefix meaning "new" or "recent"
8. 50s actress Joanne (homonym of "drew")
9. Alphabet letter before "tee"
10. Drive or urge forward
11. Characterized by using too many words
12. _____ general rule (2 wds.)
13. Voting against word
18. Optimistic; happy; cheerful
21. Actress Kirsten of "Spider-Man"
22. "Everybody Loves Raymond" TV network
23. Cheerleader's word
25. What you go to museums to see
26. "The Catcher in the _____" (J. D. Salinger novel)
27. Parts for actors
28. FedEx's biggest rival
29. Maple tree output
34. Another big name in 34 Across
37. NBA star Shaquille
39. Occupation or profession
40. Permit; allow
41. "_____ little teapot" (2 wds.)
42. Fluent; glib; talkative
44. _____ Beta Kappa (college honor society) (anagram of "hip")
45. Biblical book of Leviticus (abbr.)
46. Funeral songs or laments
48. Finishes first after all (2 wds.)
49. Inventor Whitney
50. Use your eyes
55. Small, shrimplike food of many whales
56. First American to orbit the Earth, John
59. _____ American (black American)
60. Noah's boat
61. Curly, _____, and Larry (The Three Stooges)
62. Very Important Person (abbr.)
63. "_____ day my ship will come"
64. Exact midpoint (abbr.)
65. Put to work; employ
66. Bummed out; not happy

We all get caught short from time to time. We sit there knowing we need more of something: food or money or clothes. When those times happen, when you feel as if you deserve another piece of the pie, you just want to scream: "Gimme more!"

Crossword Puzzle 19
Gimme More!

ACROSS

1. Pepper's partner
5. "Anna and the King of _____"
9. Make or become confused (anagram of "laded")
14. Robert _____ (Confederate general) (2 wds.)
15. Something you shouldn't do
16. Judge and jury event
17. Lacking; shortage (2 wds.)
19. Entice; lure
20. Tyrants or oppressors
21. _____ general rule (2 wds.)
23. Japanese figure skater Midori
24. Words or sounds of hesitation
25. "The _____ and the Pendulum"
26. Shortened reference to an unknown author
27. Connector to the Internet
30. Move from bottom to top of an e-document (2 wds.)
32. Sweet suffix with lemon or lime
33. "My country _____ of thee..."
34. Writer of verse
35. Lack or shortage, especially of money
38. Smallness of quantity; scarcity
41. Teheran's country
42. Gangster's gun (anagram of "tag")
43. Metal-bearing mineral or rock
44. Insufficiency or shortness of supply
46. Singer Tucker or actress Roberts
48. Clark Kent's Ms. Lane (anagram of "soil")
49. "One," in Spanish
50. E-cousin of "org" or "gov"
51. Do perfectly on a test
52. Biggest rival of FedEx
53. Most agile or nimble
57. Trigonometric cousins of tangents and secants
59. Not nearly enough (2 wds.)
61. Bulletin board "stickers"
62. Biblical twin brother of Jacob
63. Slang for "big amount" (2 wds.)
64. More clever or crafty
65. Baby dogs or seals
66. Require

DOWN

1. Forward an e-mail (anagram of "dens")
2. _____ vera (skin moisturizer)
3. Gives permission
4. Conical Native American dwelling
5. Supercilious people
6. Debt markers, for short
7. Director Lee of "Crouching Tiger"
8. Fabric made of Angora goat fleece
9. _____ boy!
10. Dr. of rap fame
11. Lessening; reduction
12. Carry-around kind of computer
13. Singer John of "Candle in the Wind"
18. Comedian Macdonald's "The _____ Show"
22. Conclude; terminate (2 wds.)
25. Macs, Dells, etc.
26. Oldest of the acting Baldwin brothers
27. Angry
28. "_____ on a Grecian Urn" (Keats)
29. State of lacking or incompleteness
30. Use a chair
31. Actor Diamond Philips
33. Kevin Costner movie about pro golfers (2 wds.)
36. Gershwin and Levin first names (anagram of "sari")
37. Automobile
38. Give money for work done
39. Attempt
40. Affirmative reply or vote
42. Pontiac muscle car initials (anagram of "got")
44. Friendly; gregarious; enjoying others' company
45. Arched upper surface of your foot
46. Actress Spelling of "Beverly Hills 90210"
47. Author of "The Bonesetter's Daughter" (2 wds.)
48. Endures
50. Barely better-than-average report card grade (2 wds.)
52. Russia and its satellites, before 1993 (abbr.)
53. _____ opera (daytime TV show)
54. Suffix meaning "feminine"
55. Juniper berry (anagram of "sole")
56. Be inclined toward something
58. Increase; enlarge; lengthen
60. Initials of the college Buckeyes

Groupie Puzzle 5

I U M O L D S O E

M _ _ _ _ I _ _ _

P O C Y S H I N M

_ _ M _ _ O _ _ _

T P A L G U S P N N I

_ _ _ P _ _ _ _ I _ _

X O P Y R

_ R O _ _

G Y E M T P A R A

_ A _ _ _ _ A _ _

U G O L E N

L _ _ N _ _

Groupie Phrase

R C U S C A I S H A M I L

_ _ _ I _ A _ _ _ _ _ _ _

Groupie Puzzle 6

S U M A S E

_ S _ _ E

T P E T M I I N S R E

M _ _ _ _ _ _ _ _ E _

R E R

_ _ _

Y S E I Z H O P T H E

_ _ _ O _ H _ _ _ _ _

L T E A C U P E S

_ P _ _ U _ _ _ _

G L U Y L C I O A T F

F _ _ _ _ _ L _ _ _ _

Groupie Phrase

W A D O G H E T R E N G E T I

_ _ _ _ _ _ _ R O _ _

_ _ _ _

Groupie Puzzle 7

I H I P L N N C

L _ _ _ H _ _ _

C R O N H A

_ N _ _ O _

E C O V G E R N

_ _ _ V E _ _ _

S C E E N S

E _ _ _ _ E

V A T L P I O

_ I _ _ A _

B A S E T S U N C

_ _ B _ T _ _ _ _

Groupie Phrase

X R A T F C O U R H M T T E E

C _ _ _   _ _   T _ _

_ _ _ _ _ _

Groupie Puzzle 8

D A Y R A T M N O

_ _ N _ _ T _ _ _

'S A E L S P A W O O T R O T K R H

P _ _ T _ _   _ _ _ _ _ _ _

_ _ _ _

C U S E T A N I O

_ E _ C _ _ _ _

T I T N O P E P I I C R A

_ _ _ _ I _ _ _ A _ _ _ _

L O R S A

S O _ _ _

T E E C M L N I N

I _ C _ _ _ _ _ _

Groupie Phrase

N R O H E I C O R N S E I M A

C _ _ _   _ A _ _   _ _

_ _ _ _ _

Groupie Puzzle 9

D S E R W H

S _ _ E _ _

L F A I C O S U L A

_ A L _ _ _ _ _ _ _

C L I Y T D I P U

D _ _ _ C _ _ _

A S D E I B

_ I _ S _ _

B C O S U D E R

O _ _ C _ _ _ _

C A F E D A

_ A _ _ E

Groupie Phrase

A H N D E G I D A D E N

_ I _ _ _ _ A _ _ _ _ _

Groupie Puzzle 10

O C I T D E N C E

C _ _ _ _ I _ _ _

G T H U Y A H

_ A _ _ H _ _

C T E L R R O F E

R _ _ _ _ _ _ O _

U S E I X I T Q E

_ X _ _ _ _ I _ _

E L I T V P U S R E A

S _ _ _ _ L _ _ _ _ _ _

G S U E R O G O

_ O _ _ _ O _ _

Groupie Phrase

E L R O R I M R W O H T I R
N R M R O A L

_ _ R _ _ _ _ _ _ R

_ _ _ _ _ _ _ _ _ _

Groupie Puzzle 11

X P A E R A T E S E

E _ _ _ _ E _ _ _ _

S A R S H A

_ A R _ _ _

L E E X I

_ _ I L _

U E C R R S U T T

_ _ R _ _ _ U _ _

E I C N L I N

I _ _ _ _ _ E

T N I M A D E O

_ _ _ I _ A _ _

Groupie Phrase

R W E V L A T E L U P H I D

_ _ _ _ E _ _ _ _ H _ _ _ _ _ _

Groupie Puzzle 12

A N R D E E M

_ E A _ _ _ _

F E C O S U B T A

_ _ _ U _ C _ _ _

M Y S I T E

S _ _ _ I _

P X E E L R P

_ E _ P _ _ _

Q I E C O V E U A T

_ Q U _ _ _ _ _ _ _

T W Z A L

_ A L _ _

Groupie Phrase

H U A C D S U N E E I N A O
E R S T D

_ _ _ _ _ A _ _ _ D _ _ _

_ _ _ _ _

Groupie Puzzle 13

Y A I V N T

_ _ N I _ _

L P E E N C N O O D E

P _ _ _ _ _ E _ _ _ _ _

T A Y S A F N

_ A _ _ _ S _

P A N U T O I

_ T O _ _ _ _

I T A R O T N A M U

_ _ _ U _ A _ _ _ _

C E E S E B N U C P

P _ _ E _ _ _ _ _

Groupie Phrase

Y T O H T O U U N A F I O N F

_ O _ _ _ _ I _ _ _ _ _ _ _ _

Cryptofamily Puzzle 29

He Got Up on the Wrong Side of the Bed

Z V T U U
G R U F F

Y X C E X C J W V B T M

Y V X C J G

B K M E F C X E W

S W N F C Z

R T W V T A B T M

Q W V S W V M W

Q W W S F M O

F V X M Y F K A W

Y B C E W C E F B T M

Y O T V A F M O

Y X A A B T M

X C C B G F C Z

Q W E T A X C E

B V C W V G

Cryptofamily Puzzle 30
Oh, My Gosh. Look at That!

M L X Z B Y Z K X
S P E C T A C L E

J Y J C B V

E Y J Q X K

E C J Y Z K X

X A Z X L B C H W

L T X W H E X W H W

S H W F X J

M D J L J C M X

M T H Z G

L J H F C R V

X W C R E Y

Z D J C H M C B V

H F F C B V

L Y J Y R H W

E Y M B X J L C X Z X

Cryptofamily Puzzle 31
A Little Bit Here, a Little Bit There . . .

I Q G C W N W S K G W
C O N S T I T U E N T

I T O S C K

N G M X K Y N K G W

U X O M E K G W

U X O I W N Q G

I O W K M Q X L

O T T Q W E K G W

J X O G I D

E Q X C K T

K T K E K G W

Y N Z N C N Q G

Y K A O X W E K G W

A Q X W N Q G

Y K W X N W S C

I Q E A Q G K G W

Cryptofamily Puzzle 32
Free at Last!

M W B S G H R B D M
E M A N C I P A T E

X S O H S Y

J H O M Q B D M

X S T E B G I J M

Y M Q M F X J B D M

M P D Q H G B D M

R B Q U J M

X S J M B T E

Q M J M B T M

Y H T G E B Q F M

B G C X H D

Q M T G X M

Q M Y M M W

Q M R Q H M A M

Y M J H A M Q

Cryptofamily Puzzle 33
Hey, I Was Here First!

W P L Q M M E
P I O N E E R

W E M O K E R L E

F V E I P Q A M E

B L E M S L E H

W E L U L A K M

W E M Z L Q P C P L Q

W E M D K M U

X V Q A K V E H

W E M M Z W C P L Q

V Q C M O M H M Q O M

W E M U K H M

L X M E C K E M

W E M H P O C P L Q

C E V P U I U V Y M E

C E M Q H R M C C M E

Cryptofamily Puzzle 34
Undercover Work

O R U X Q P P G D Q G D
S U B T E R R A N E A N

V L S Q P X

J B U Q P D G X B D I

B D S B O B U Y Q

O Q F R Q O X Q P Q A

O R U V L D O V B L R O

A L P N G D X

Y G X Q D X

F R B Q O V Q D X

B N W Q D Q X P G U Y Q

L U O V R P Q

O Q V Y R A Q A

O R U Y B N B D G Y

R D N G D B H Q O X Q A

Y R P E B D I

Cryptofamily Puzzle 35
Let's Get Something Going

Z P F R T H W P Y
S T I M U L A T E

F R L Y H

L I K L W S W P Y

Z F I Y

X K R L Y H

E K R Y Q P

L I Y X F L F P W P Y

F Q W T S T I W P Y

F Q Z P F S W P Y

G I K W X J

E K Z P Y I

M F Q V H Y

G Y S Y P

X T H P F O W P Y

P Y R L P

Cryptofamily Puzzle 36
Like a Rock

H Y D C F J U S W P D
P R E D I C T A B L E

J S P T

F M C D Q U Y A J U F W P D

Q U D S C B S Q U

C A Y S W P D

F Y Y D G D Y Q F W P D

F M B P D V F W P D

D M U Y D M J K D C

F T H D Y U A Y W S W P D

F T T A U S W P D

F M D V U F M E A F Q K S W P D

H D Y H D U A S P

H D Y D M M F S P

F M C D P F W P D

W S P S M J D C

Cryptofamily Puzzle 37
Keeping It Brief

Y U Z R H W S W B J
A B R I D G M E N T

R Z H W Q J

E Y Y U W X Z E J Z C B

Q V S S E U O

Q O B C F Q Z Q

Q V U X W O

E Y Q J U E M J

C V J P Z B W

Q A W J M T

R Z E H U E S

R W P Z B W E J Z C B

M C B R W B Q E J Z C B

M C B J U E M J Z C B

Q Z P T C V W J J W

M C B J C V U

Cryptofamily Puzzle 38
Flowery Talk

H N C I F V U P W
G A R N I S H E D

H F M W P W

L V E P I E N E F L B V

H N B W Z

P G E C N O N H N I E

U Z Y P C D L M F K

D P T P R P M P W

P Q D P M M F V U P W

W P K L C N E F O P

L C I N E P

N J J P K E P W

Y L Q Y L B V

H C N I W F L V P

N W L C I P W

P I U N I K P W

Cryptofamily Puzzle 39
Can We Talk?

R H E T W Q I P O C
H O S P I T A B L E

Z C K W I O

A H J T I K W H K I P O C

N U P I K C

I J W I P O C

Z U C Z I U W H N E

C F Q U H L C U Q C G

X H L W I O

A H U G W I O

A H J J N K W A I Q W L C

I J W A I P O C

E H A W I P O C

A R I U W E J I Q W A

A H K L W L W I O

H N Q Z H W K Z

Cryptofamily Puzzle 40
It's Loud in Here!

G A L B C U O V P
S T R I D E N C Y

C B O

L U Q U L J U L N A B S O

V N V D B O O N A B S O

V T N O X S L

V L U G V U O C S

I N O I N L U

A W F W T A

Q S V B I U L N A B S O

W T W T N A B S O

J U C T N F

M N O C U F S O B W F

A W L F S B T

J S F J N L C F U O A

V T N F S L

Cryptofamily Puzzle 41
Hey, Lazarus!

H D L D H S L I G
I N A N I M A T E

W L I L Z

V G X G L B G V

V G S H B G V

C A G L I O Z G B B

S Y A H C E D V

K G A H B O H D Q

G T I H D X I

Z G I O L Z

I G A S H D L Z

X L V L U G A Y E B

Z H U H V

K L Z Z H V

V G W E D X I

Z H W G Z G B B

END NOTE

You are a hard worker! You have proven your brains and your perseverance by making it this far in *SAT Vocabulary Express*. You have completed all the chapters containing the medium and medium-to-hard vocabulary and puzzles. Now it is your chance to really shine. We warn you. The puzzles from here on are not for the faint of heart, but they will challenge and intrigue you. You have all the tools you need to break the code on any question on the new SAT that has tough vocabulary. Get ready to strut your stuff. The next puzzles may take more than one attempt, but we think you will be able to plow through them. And, who knows? Perhaps you are now as hooked on puzzles as we are!

Fun Quiz

The following Cryptofamily puzzle contains the names of famous couples throughout history and from famous books and plays. Can you figure them out? We have not given you any clues to help you get started. Try to think of as many couples as you can. Do any of the names have double letters or obvious repeating patterns? Look for those names first, and then continue from there.

Cryptofamily Puzzle 42
Famous Couples

H E I Y J & K J E Y V X F J

E I Y S I L & F W J S Z E Y V E

J V S B & Z B L F C J

P J V Y V N H J   B Y J X I & E W X F J   K   Y S G W E B

R E I J   J L V J & J H M E V I I   V S F C J B Y J V

Z E V X B & C J W J I

C J E Y C F W X A A & F E Y C L

F E V S W L I   K J B B J Y Y J & R S C I   G J I I J H L

V S Q J S & R N W X J Y

E I I E   G E V J I X I E & E W J G B J X   U V S I B G X

I E Z S W J S I & R S B J Z C X I J

B F E V W J Y Y   S ' C E V E & V C J Y Y   K N Y W J V

W E I F J W S Y & P N X I J U J V J

B S I I L & F C J V

H E U X H & K E Y C B C J K E

W E H L   H X E I E & Z V X I F J   F C E V W J B

Chapter 9

CHALLENGING PUZZLES

Traditionally, the hardest *New York Times* crossword puzzle of the week appears on Saturday. These puzzles are even harder than the much larger Sunday crosswords. One of the reasons why they're harder is that they have no theme: There are no cues or clues from other answers to help you with the longer answer words or phrases.

We have here a challenging crossword for you hardy souls who've made it this far. You know who you are. You're SAT code-breaking grandmasters, and here's your chance to see if you can piece a few difficult words together, just as you will on the SAT when your time comes. It's a themeless crossword puzzle, or what we call a vocabulary builder.

Crossword Puzzle 20
A Vocabulary Builder

ACROSS

1. On _____ (without a contract)
5. Rubbed the wrong away?
11. Unruly crowd
14. Othello's evil lieutenant
15. Woman of Hispanic heritage
16. In existence
17. Published or proclaimed formally
19. Had the pack at one's heels
20. Junior year exam, for short
21. Medieval mauler
23. Kind of TV or modem
26. Characterized by a pretentious manner
29. Lyric poems
32. Musical instrument of the reed family
33. Graphic or centric prefix
34. Show those pearly whites
35. Clumsy oaf
38. Not expressly stated but there
40. Having a warlike character
42. Uses as a platform (2 wds.)
44. More sharply defined
47. Constituent members
48. Spider's specialty
50. Bustle; fuss
51. Assistant; helper
52. Miami, Florida's county
53. Krispy Kreme delight
54. Not doing much of anything
56. Sound of surprise
58. Honest _____
60. Attackers of cherished beliefs
66. Ares or Mars's domain
67. One of Illinois's Quad Cities
68. "Saturday Night Live" offering
69. Actors Begley and Begley, Jr.
70. Aspiring doctor's major
71. Ratio in a right triangle

DOWN

1. Small drink
2. Average, to a golfer
3. What a braggart displays
4. Fitted in to make perfect
5. Fitzgerald of jazz fame
6. Made of mixed elements
7. _____ loss for words (2 wds.)
8. Take a chair
9. Foe
10. Mama's mate
11. Curse or imprecation
12. Gold mine product
13. Pajamas are worn here
18. Put to work
22. Transpiring; eventuating (3 wds.)
23. He gives orders to a maj.
24. _____ Dhabi (country)
25. Specialists in a B-52
27. Ruled the kingdom
28. Weighty book
30. Inventor Whitney
31. Harden in cement, e.g.
34. Snow racer
36. Inventor of a self-named auto
37. T-shirts for big, big people (abbr.)
39. Syllable meaning "before"
41. The Hawkeye State
42. Masseuse's work spot
43. _____ chi (exercise form)
45. Alternative to .com or .org
46. Decay
49. Depart (2 wds.)
52. Home ornamentation
53. Internet connector
55. Flaccid; lacking firmness
57. Did this puzzle perfectly!
58. Overwhelming admiration
59. Not good
61. Bullfight cheer
62. Two-player, pencil-and-paper game
63. Hit the slopes
64. Element abbreviated Sn
65. Title bestowed on Theresa of Avila (abbr.)

Anagram Magic Square Puzzle 10

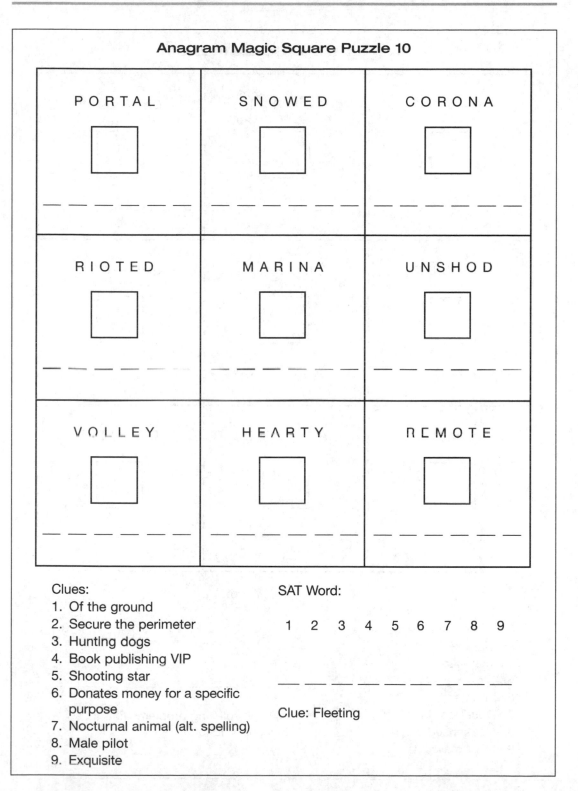

PORTAL	SNOWED	CORONA
RIOTED	MARINA	UNSHOD
VOLLEY	HEARTY	REMOTE

Clues:
1. Of the ground
2. Secure the perimeter
3. Hunting dogs
4. Book publishing VIP
5. Shooting star
6. Donates money for a specific purpose
7. Nocturnal animal (alt. spelling)
8. Male pilot
9. Exquisite

SAT Word:

1 2 3 4 5 6 7 8 9

___ ___ ___ ___ ___ ___ ___ ___ ___

Clue: Fleeting

Anagram Magic Square Puzzle 11

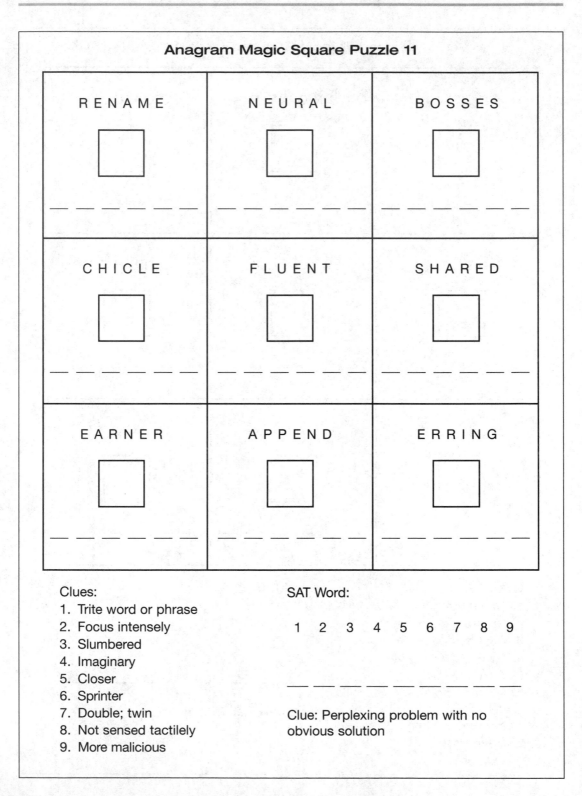

R E N A M E	N E U R A L	B O S S E S
C H I C L E	F L U E N T	S H A R E D
E A R N E R	A P P E N D	E R R I N G

Clues:
1. Trite word or phrase
2. Focus intensely
3. Slumbered
4. Imaginary
5. Closer
6. Sprinter
7. Double; twin
8. Not sensed tactilely
9. More malicious

SAT Word:

1 2 3 4 5 6 7 8 9

— — — — — — — — —

Clue: Perplexing problem with no obvious solution

These are the challenging puzzles, so only words with four or more letters count toward the score! The answer key presents the combined effort of several people with too much time on their hands.

Word within Word Puzzle 4

an·thro·po·cen·trism (an´thrə pō sen´triz əm), *n.*
a human theory or view.

Best score so far: 561

Word within Word Puzzle 5

cir·cum·lo·cu·tion (sûr´kəm lō kyoo´shən), *n.*

1. a roundabout or indirect way of speaking; the use of more words than necessary to express an idea.

2. a roundabout expression.

Best score so far: 167

Word within Word Puzzle 6

dis·in·gen·u·ous (dis´in jen´yoo əs), *adj.*

1. lacking in frankness, candor, or sincerity; falsely or hypocritically ingenuous; insincere: *Her excuse was rather disingenuous.*

Best score so far: 52

Word within Word Puzzle 7

e·quiv·o·cate (i kwiv´ə kāt´), *v.i.,* **-cat·ed, -cat·ing.**

1. to use ambiguous or unclear expressions, usually to avoid commitment or in order to mislead; prevaricate or hedge: *When asked directly for his position on disarmament, the candidate only equivocated.*

Best score so far: 26

Word within Word Puzzle 8

lo·qua·cious (lō kwā´shəs), *adj.*

1. talking or tending to talk much or freely; talkative; chattering; babbling; garrulous: *a loquacious dinner guest.*

2. characterized by excessive talk; wordy: *easily the most loquacious play of the season.*

Best score so far: 18

Word within Word Puzzle 9

mach·i·na·tion (mak´ə nā´shən), *n.*

1. an act or instance of machinating.

2. usually, *machinations.* crafty schemes; plots; intrigues.

Best score so far: 116

Quotation Puzzle 9

1P	2N	3F	4K	5G		6Q	7K	8G	9M	10A	11J		12Q	13P	14N	15G	16D
17F		18D	19J	20K		21D	22I	23Q	24B	25F	26J	27C	28K		29B	30P	31H
32J	33G	34C		35D	36O	37M	38K		39P	40C	41N	42M	43F	44H	45D	46O	47L
	48A	49E	50I		51N	52L	53E	54D	55A	56J	57C	58M		59A	60B	61I	
62M	63C	64P	65O		66F	67L	68P	69H	70G	71B	72I	73O		74C	75D	76O	77Q
78B	79L	80K		81I	82H	83N	84F	85P	86B	87L	88O	89J		90O	91C	92F	93G
	94N	95G	96P	97E	98K	99I	100B		101L	102N		103N	104K	105B	106O	107G	108J
109L		110B	111L	112G	113F		114Q	115E	116B	117H	118D		119P	120C	121G	122D	123Q
124B	125K	126L	127E		128D	129C	130O	131L	132A	133E	134Q						

Clues:

A. Flying elephant of Disney fame

10 132 55 48 59

B. English actress of "Punch-Drunk Love" (2 wds.)

110 86 78 116 100 124 71 24 29 105 60

C. Extremely wicked or villainous

27 57 74 120 63 91 129 40 34

D. 98 Degree member, J. Simpson's husband (2 wds.)

45 18 128 16 122 75 21 35 54 118

E. Protected from disease by a shot

115 133 53 49 127 97

F Spaceships like "Atlantis" and "Discovery"

113 25 66 84 43 92 3 17

G. Bummed out and gloomy; depressed

70 33 121 112 15 8 107 95 93 5

H. Rome's country

69 82 44 117 31

I. The _____ thing (all the rage)

22 99 72 61 81 50

J. Beatles #1 rereleased "Naked" in 2003 (3 wds.)

32 108 89 26 19 56 11

K. Causes or gives rise to

38 104 28 125 80 98 7 4 20

L. Head general, Confederate Army, Civil War (3 wds.)

111 79 101 52 109 131 126 67 47 87

M. All night parties

58 9 37 62 42

N. Tending to annoy or cause ill will

83 41 51 103 94 14 2 102

O. Nightly work for Dan Rather, Tom Brokaw, etc.

88 73 90 76 46 36 65 106 130

P. England's principal waterway (2 wds.)

30 119 1 68 13 64 96 85 39

Q. Calmed; comforted; tranquilized

114 123 23 12 77 134 6

Quotation Puzzle 10

1B	2A	■	3Q	4A	5M	■	6H	7J	8C	9F	■	10G	11L	12U	■	13F	14S
15Q	16E	17U	18D	19R	20P	21B	22J	■	23A	24K	25U	26H	27S	28I	29B	■	30I
31S	32D	33E	34R	35Q	36T	■	37M	38F	39K	■	40A	41Q	42B	43I	44G	45D	■
46H	47E	48Q	49B	50F	51K	52M	53S	54C	55U	56R	57L	■	58E	59U	60H	■	61C
62H	63O	64L	65M	66P	■	67U	68F	■	69A	70K	71C	■	72B	73Q	74R	■	75M
76B	77Q	78K	79O	■	80G	81T	82O	83H	84N	85A	■	86F	87H	88L	89P	90U	91N
■	92I	93L	94H	■	95L	96H	■	97D	■	98J	99O	100D	101S	102P	■	103J	104F
105B	106T	107N	■	108T	109M	110E	111A	112N	113K	■	114C	115I	116S	117H	■	118U	119S
120P	121L	122U	123B	■	124F	125L	126U	127J	128K	■	129C	130T	■	131E	■	132T	133D
134G	135O	■	136E	137G	■	138N	139J	140L	141T	142D	143S	144O	145P	146F	147U	148R	■

Clues:

A. Comedian teamed with Bing Crosby in movies (2 wds.)

‾23‾ ‾2‾ ‾69‾ ‾40‾ ‾4‾ ‾111‾ ‾85‾

B. Effrontery; inclination to talk back

‾72‾ ‾42‾ ‾49‾ ‾76‾ ‾1‾ ‾123‾ ‾29‾ ‾21‾ ‾105‾

C. Sir Thomas _____ (man famous for importing tea to U.S.)

‾114‾ ‾129‾ ‾61‾ ‾71‾ ‾8‾ ‾54‾

D. Sideways pass in football

‾133‾ ‾97‾ ‾45‾ ‾142‾ ‾18‾ ‾100‾ ‾32‾

E. Nickname for the Wild West's Bill Cody

‾136‾ ‾47‾ ‾16‾ ‾58‾ ‾131‾ ‾33‾ ‾110‾

F. Director of the movie "A Beautiful Mind" (2 wds.)

‾86‾ ‾124‾ ‾38‾ ‾104‾ ‾68‾ ‾9‾ ‾146‾ ‾50‾ ‾13‾

G. Ingredient that makes bread rise

‾137‾ ‾44‾ ‾134‾ ‾80‾ ‾10‾

H. Big 7-day period for the Nielsen TV ratings (2 wds.)

‾96‾ ‾26‾ ‾87‾ ‾117‾ ‾83‾ ‾46‾ ‾60‾ ‾94‾ ‾62‾ ‾6‾

I. Popeye's girlfriend

‾92‾ ‾43‾ ‾115‾ ‾30‾ ‾28‾

J. Huey, Dewey, or Louie, to Donald Duck

‾7‾ ‾22‾ ‾98‾ ‾139‾ ‾127‾ ‾103‾

K. Learned or scholarly; having great knowledge

‾113‾ ‾128‾ ‾70‾ ‾39‾ ‾51‾ ‾78‾ ‾24‾

L. Basic or natural aversion; repugnance

‾88‾ ‾93‾ ‾125‾ ‾95‾ ‾64‾ ‾140‾ ‾121‾ ‾11‾ ‾57‾

M. Spill the beans; rat on; tattle

‾52‾ ‾75‾ ‾5‾ ‾109‾ ‾37‾ ‾65‾

N. Shouts out loud

‾91‾ ‾107‾ ‾112‾ ‾84‾ ‾138‾

O. Hire a person for a job

‾79‾ ‾82‾ ‾144‾ ‾99‾ ‾63‾ ‾135‾

P. Sewing or stitching necessity

‾20‾ ‾102‾ ‾145‾ ‾120‾ ‾89‾ ‾66‾

Q. Give pleasure to a person; delight; gladden

‾35‾ ‾48‾ ‾41‾ ‾73‾ ‾77‾ ‾15‾ ‾3‾

R. Contract an apartment renter must sign

‾56‾ ‾19‾ ‾34‾ ‾74‾ ‾148‾

S. Penetrating; cutting; trenchant

‾31‾ ‾119‾ ‾101‾ ‾14‾ ‾143‾ ‾53‾ ‾116‾ ‾27‾

T. Gilligan's TV "boss"

‾130‾ ‾141‾ ‾81‾ ‾132‾ ‾108‾ ‾36‾ ‾106‾

U. Aussie actor in "The Patriot" and "A Knight's Tale" (2 wds.)

‾122‾ ‾12‾ ‾118‾ ‾25‾ ‾126‾ ‾90‾ ‾17‾ ‾67‾ ‾55‾ ‾59‾ ‾147‾

This puzzle provides little in the way of clues, making it the most difficult hidden meanings puzzle. It will take more time, but we think you will be able to figure it out!

Hidden Meanings Puzzle 14

ar·cha·ic (är kā´ik), *adj.*

1. _____(6) by the _____(15) of an _____(7) _____(6); _____(10).

ed·i·fy (ed´ə fī), *v.t.,* **-fied, -fy·ing.**

1. to _____(8) or _____(7), especially _____(7) or _____(11); _____(6).

gre·gar·i·ous (gri gâr´ē əs), *adj.*

1. _____(4) of the _____(7) of _____(6); _____(8).

pe·jo·ra·tive (pi jôr´ə tiv, -jor´-, pej´ə rā´, pē´jə-), *adj.*

1. having a _____(11), _____(10), or _____(10) _____(6) or _____(5).

ver·nac·u·lar (vər nak´yə lər, və nak´-), *adj.*

1. (of language) _____(6) or _____(10) as [_____(7) to _____(8) or _____(7)].

per·il·ous (per´ə ləs), *adj.*

1. _____(9) or _____(4) of _____(5) _____(4) or _____(5); _____(9); _____(9).

rev·e·la·tion (rev´ə lā´shən), *n.*

1. the act of _____(9) or _____(10); _____(10).

bi·as (bī´əs), *n., adj., adv., v.,* **bi·ased, bi·as·ing** or (*especially British*) **bi·assed, bi·as·sing.** —*n.*

1. an _____(7) or _____(8) line of _____(9), especially _____(6) a _____(5) _____(6).

2. a particular _____(8) or _____(11), especially one who prevents _____(12) _____(13) of a _____(8); _____(9).

dearth (dûrth), *n.*

1. an _____(10) _____(6); _____(8); _____(4).

im·pec·ca·ble (im pek´ə bəl), *adj.*

1. _____(9); _____(8); _____(14).

Hidden Meanings Puzzle 14 *(continued)*

4 LETTERS	7 LETTERS	10 LETTERS
FOND	OBLIQUE	DISCLOSURE
RISK	EARLIER	DEROGATORY
LACK	MORALLY	INDIGENOUS
FULL	OPPOSED	INADEQUATE
	BENEFIT	DISCLOSING
5 LETTERS	COMPANY	ANTIQUATED
FORCE	LEARNED	BELITTLING
WOVEN		
PERIL	8 LETTERS	11 LETTERS
GRAVE	SOCIABLE	INCLINATION
	DIAGONAL	SPIRITUALLY
6 LETTERS	QUESTION	DISPARAGING
ACROSS	SCARCITY	
NATIVE	LITERARY	12 LETTERS
PERIOD	INSTRUCT	UNPREJUDICED
FABRIC	TENDENCY	
MARKED	FLAWLESS	13 LETTERS
UPLIFT		CONSIDERATION
SUPPLY	9 LETTERS	
OTHERS	DIRECTION	14 LETTERS
EFFECT	DANGEROUS	IRREPROACHABLE
	INVOLVING	
	FAULTLESS	15 LETTERS
	REVEALING	CHARACTERISTICS
	PREJUDICE	
	HAZARDOUS	

Some words in a particular definition will be interchangeable.

CLOSING LETTER TO STUDENTS

Dear Students:

Congratulations! You are now ready to crack the code of the vocabulary in the new SAT. You have learned many new words but, more importantly, you have learned how to play with words, how to build them and pull them apart, and how to use their connotations to help you guess well on the SAT.

People will try to tell you how difficult the SAT is and how nervous you should be. They are entitled to their opinion. But you don't have to be afraid, because you know the SAT is a game that you can win. Yes, the test is hard, but you are no slouch. You can handle it. No test is going to make you give up. Take the SAT challenge. Stand tall, put on your game face, and kick some butt.

The same people who tell you that the SAT is going to be scary will also tell you that it is impossible to get into a good school. Although it is a little more competitive at the top colleges and universities than it used to be, it is not impossible. Students are admitted every year. Why not you? Do the best job you can on the SAT and in your application. Make sure you apply to two safety schools that you would be happy to attend and then relax and enjoy your senior year. There is no one perfect college for you. You can be happy and get a wonderful education at any number of colleges. If you really hate where you end up, you can transfer.

A 1600 on the SAT will not guarantee you a spot at an Ivy League school. This means that many people with less than perfect scores are admitted to Ivy League schools. And many students from less than top schools are admitted to the top graduate schools every year. Only your undergraduate transcript will be evaluated when you apply to graduate school, so it will matter how well you do in college, not how well your college is ranked in *U.S. News and World*

Report. The college you attend may influence your first job opportunity, but only your success and work ethic at your first job will get you a better second job.

Deciding where to apply and where to attend college are big decisions, but they are not the biggest or the most important decisions you will ever make in your life. You can grow, learn, and explore life at any college or university in the world.

Good luck,

Jacqueline Byrne

Michael Ashley

Answers

Crossword Puzzle 1

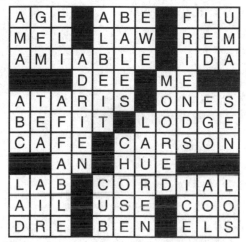

Easy Going

Crossword Puzzle 2

All Talk

Crossword Puzzle 3

Puzzle You—Not!

Quotation Puzzle 1

Quote: *"If you can't beat them, arrange to have them beaten."* George Carlin.

Answers: **A.** BABE RUTH, **B.** VENERATE, **C.** THE RING, **D.** RACCOON, **E.** ENMITY, **F.** EAGLE, **G.** AGATE, **H.** FATHOM.

Quotation Puzzle 2

Quote: *"Do you think my mind is maturing late, or simply rotted early?"* Ogden Nash.

Answers: **A.** ATHENS, **B.** TURMOIL, **C.** HANSON, **D.** IGLOO, **E.** SYNONYM, **F.** MADRID, **G.** TRULY, **H.** GRADE, **I.** KITTY, **J.** IMPEDE.

Anagram Magic Square Puzzle 1

1. Padre, **2.** Anger, **3.** Route, **4,** Askew, **5.** Melon, **6.** Optic, **7.** Urban, **8.** Night, **9.** Tiara.
SAT Word: Paramount.

Anagram Magic Square 2

1. Verse, **2.** Aloft, **3.** Coops, **4.** Idler, **5.** Leaks, **6.** Lease, **7.** Alert, **8.** Truce, **9.** Exalt.
SAT Word: Vacillate.

CHAPTER 2 ANSWERS

Hidden Meanings Puzzle 1

subtle 1. thin, <u>tenuous</u>, or rarefied, as a fluid or an odor. **2.** fine or <u>delicate</u> in meaning or intent; <u>difficult</u> to perceive or understand. **3.** delicate or faint and <u>mysterious</u>. **viable 1.** capable of <u>living</u>. **accent 1.** <u>prominence</u> of a syllable in terms of differential loudness, or of <u>pitch</u>, or <u>length</u>, or of a combination of these. **fruitless 1.** <u>useless</u>; unproductive, without <u>results</u> or success. **2.** bearing no fruit, <u>barren</u>. **reserve 1.** to keep back or <u>save</u> for future use, <u>disposal</u>, treatment, and so on. **drawback 1.** a <u>hindrance</u> or disadvantage; an undesirable or <u>objectionable</u> feature. **homogeneous 1.** composed of parts or <u>elements</u> that are all of the same kind; not <u>heterogeneous</u>. **2.** of the same kind or <u>nature</u>; essentially <u>alike</u>. **receptive 1.** having the quality of <u>receiving</u>, taking in, or <u>admitting</u>. **2.** able or quick to receive knowledge, <u>ideas</u>, and so on. **genre 1.** a class or <u>category</u> of <u>artistic</u> endeavor having a particular form, content, technique, or the like. **respite 1.** a delay or <u>cessation</u> for a time, especially of anything <u>distressing</u> or trying; an <u>interval</u> of relief.

Hidden Meanings Puzzle 2

surpass 1. to go <u>beyond</u> in amount, extent, or degree; to be greater than; <u>exceed</u> **2.** to go beyond in excellence or achievement; be superior to; <u>excel</u>. **diction 1.** <u>style</u> of speaking or writing as dependent upon <u>choice</u> of words. **2.** the accent, inflection, <u>intonation</u>, and speech-sound quality manifested by an individual speaker, usually judged in terms of prevailing standards of acceptability; **genuine 1.** possessing the claimed or <u>attributed</u> character, quality, or origin; not <u>counterfeit</u>; <u>authentic</u>. **tentative 1.** of the nature of or made or done as a trial, <u>experiment</u>, or attempt. **2.** unsure; <u>uncertain</u>; not definite or positive; <u>hesitant</u>. **docile 1.** <u>easily</u> managed or handled; <u>tractable</u>. **2.** readily <u>trained</u> or taught; teachable. **comply 1.** to act or be in <u>accordance</u> with wishes, <u>requests</u>, demands, requirements, conditions, and so on; <u>agree</u> (sometimes followed by *with*). **revert 1.** to <u>return</u> to a former habit, practice, <u>belief</u>, condition, and so on. **2.** *Law:* to go back to or return to the former owner or to his or her <u>heirs</u>. **3.** *Biology:* to return to an earlier or <u>primitive</u> type. **assent 1.** to agree or <u>concur</u>; subscribe to (often followed by *to*). **2.** to give in; concede; yield. **devoid 1.** not <u>possessing</u>, untouched by, <u>void</u> or destitute (usually followed by *of*). **2.** to deplete or <u>strip</u> of some quality or <u>substance</u>. **seclude 1.** to place in or <u>withdraw</u> into <u>solitude</u>; remove from social contact and activity. **2.** to <u>isolate</u>; shut off; keep <u>apart</u>.

Cryptofamily Puzzle 1

APATHY, LASSITUDE, LANGUOR, LETHARGIC, SOPORIFIC, TORPOR, COMATOSE, STUPOR, PASSIVE, LISTLESS, PHLEGMATIC, SOMNOLENT, LANGUID, SLUGGISH.

Cryptofamily Puzzle 2

MALLEABLE, AMBIVALENT, VACILLATE, OBEDIENT, ABEYANCE, AMENABLE, BIDDABLE, COMPLIANT, TRACTABLE, DEFERENTIAL, OBSEQUIOUS, SERVILE, ACQUIESCENT, RESIGNED.

Cryptofamily Puzzle 3

EXHAUSTIVE, METICULOUS, SCRUPULOUS, PRAGMATIC, THOROUGHNESS, PAINSTAKING, OBSERVANT, COMPULSIVE, DILIGENT, ASSIDUOUS, OBSESSIVE, ATTENTIVE, SEDULOUS, CAREFUL.

Cryptofamily Puzzle 4

OBSTINATE, TENACIOUS, DOGGED, INTRACTABLE, INTRANSIGENT, PERVERSE, WILLFUL, OBSTREPEROUS, BULLHEADED, OBDURATE, PUGNACIOUS, DOGMATIC, INCORRIGIBLE, PIGHEADED.

Groupie Puzzle 1

premeditate, justified, revenge, biblical, optical, retaliate. Eye for an eye.

Groupie Puzzle 2

glassy, serene, horizontal, two-dimensional, breakfast, off-key. Flat as a pancake.

CHAPTER 3 ANSWERS

Word Creation Puzzle 1

tenant	projection	confer
tension	injection	infertile
retain	conjection	refer
aver	rejection	infer
veracity	reject	generate
convert	conjecture	generic
reverse	component	generation
averse	compose	progenerate
conversant	repose	regenerate
aversion	propose	fiction
reversion	impose	confection
conversation	posture	infection
manual	current	factual
manufacture	cursory	prefect
many	recurrent	factory
inject	concurrent	faction
project	fertile	

Word within Word Puzzle 1

FRACTIOUS—9 letters

act	cart	fast
actor	cast	fat
afro	cat	fiat
aft	ciao	ficus
air	coat	first
aortic	coif	fist
arc	craft	focus
ascot	crust	fort
astir	curt	frat
auric	fair	iota
auto	far	oaf
car	fart	oats

our	rout	stair
oust	rust	star
out	rustic	stria
raft	sat	surf
rat	scarf	tofu
ratio	scat	turf
rift	sofa	
riot	sot	

58 words

Word within Word Puzzle 2

COMPRESSION—11 letters

cession	miser	rose
coins	miss	rosin
come	moon	scion
compose	mope	scone
compress	more	scoop
cone	moss	scope
cons	nose	score
coop	pore	scrip
cope	pose	semipro
core	press	sensor
corm	prion	sermon
corn	promlse	simper
cosine	prone	sin
cosmos	prose	sine
cress	remiss	sip
crimp	resin	sir
croon	rinse	siren
crop	rip	snip
impress	ripe	snore
income	rise	some
ion	roe	soon
iron	romp	sore
mess	room	sperm
mire	rope	spin

| spine | sponsor | spore |
| spire | spoon | |

77 words

Word within Word Puzzle 3

FACSIMILE—9 letters

ace	families	malice
ail	file	meal
aim	film	mica
aisle	flame	mice
ale	flies	mile
cafe	lace	misfile
calf	lame	sail
came	leaf	sale
case	leis	same
clime	lice	seal
elf	lies	seam
face	life	self
facile	lime	semi
fail	mace	simile
false	mail	smile
fame	male	

47 words

Phobia Puzzle 1

1. e, **2.** s, **3.** f, **4.** v, **5.** k, **6.** z, **7.** c, **8.** u, **9.** b, **10.** r, **11.** x, **12.** a, **13.** j, **14.** h, **15.** p, **16.** y, **17.** l, **18.** n, **19.** d, **20.** g, **21.** w, **22.** i, **23.** q, **24.** t, **25.** m, **26.** o.

CHAPTER 4 ANSWERS

Crossword Puzzle 4

Destructive Tendencies

Crossword Puzzle 5

Mine, All Mine!

Crossword Puzzle 6

Our House (Is a Very, Very, Very Fine House)

Anagram Magic Square Puzzle 3

1. Needs, **2.** Olive, **3.** Coins, **4.** Tough, **5.** Until, **6.** Regal, **7.** Nudes, **8.** Aster, **9.** Lapse.
SAT Word: Nocturnal.

Anagram Magic Square Puzzle 4

1. Purse, **2.** Evict, **3.** Neigh, **4.** Ideal, **5.** Nears, **6.** Stare, **7.** Untie, **8.** Leapt, **9.** Adept.
SAT Word: Peninsula.

Anagram Magic Square Puzzle 5

1. Addle, **2.** Trash, **3.** Terse, **4.** Ether, **5.** Naked, **6.** Urban, **7.** Aside, **8.** Toned, **9.** Edify.
SAT Word: Attenuate.

Anagram Magic Square Puzzle 6

1. Froth, **2.** Regal, **3.** Auger, **4.** Coals, **5.** Throw, **6.** Items, 7. Overt, **8.** Urges, **9.** South.
SAT Word: Fractious.

Hidden Meanings Puzzle 3

somber 1. gloomily dark; shadowy; dimly lighted. **2.** dark and dull, as color, or as things in respect
to color. **vocation 1.** a particular occupation, business, or profession; calling. **2.** a strong impulse or
inclination to follow a particular activity or career. **malediction 1.** a curse; imprecation. **2.** the utterance
of a curse. **provocative 1.** tending or serving to provoke; inciting, stimulating, irritating, or vexing.
vociferous 1. crying out noisily; clamorous. **infraction 1.** breach; violation; infringement. **sublime
1.** elevated or lofty in thought, language. **2.** impressing the mind with a sense of grandeur or power;
inspiring awe or veneration. **abdicate 1.** to renounce or relinquish a throne, right, power, claim,
responsibility, or the like, especially in a formal manner. **transgress 1.** to violate a law, command, moral
code, and so on; offend; sin. **2.** to pass over or go beyond a limit or boundary. **prodigy 1.** a person,
especially a child or young person, having extraordinary talent or ability. **3.** something wonderful or
marvelous; a wonder.

Hidden Meanings Puzzle 4

postscript 1. a paragraph, phrase, and the like added to a letter that has already been concluded
and signed by the writer. **sanctify 1.** to make holy; set apart as sacred; consecrate. **2.** to purify or
free from sin. **quest 1.** a search or pursuit made in order to find or obtain something. **2.** Medieval
romance. an adventurous expedition undertaken by a knight or knights to secure or achieve something.
execrable 1. utterly detestable; abominable; abhorrent. **prolix 1.** extended to great, unnecessary,
or tedious length; long and wordy. **querulous 1.** full of complaints; complaining. **2.** characterized by
or uttered in complaint; peevish. **empathy 1.** the intellectual identification with or vicarious experiencing of the feelings, thoughts, or attitudes of another. **disparage 1.** to speak of or treat slightingly;
depreciate; belittle. **2.** to bring reproach upon or discredit; lower the estimation of. **circuitous 1.**
roundabout; not direct. **diffident 1.** lacking confidence in one's own ability, worth, or fitness; timid;
shy. **2.** restrained or reserved in manner, conduct, and so on.

Hidden Meanings Puzzle 5

vilify 1. to speak ill of; defame; slander. **whet 1.** to sharpen (a knife, tool, etc.) by grinding or friction.
2. to make keen or eager; stimulate. **spurn 1.** to reject with disdain; scorn. **2.** to treat with contempt;
despise. **vibrant 1.** moving to and fro rapidly; vibrating. **2.** vibrating so as to produce sound, as a
string. **abridge 1.** to shorten by omissions while retaining the basic content. **2.** to reduce or
lessen in duration, scope, authority, and so on; diminish. **daunt 1.** to overcome with fear; intimidate.
2. to lessen the courage of; dishearten. **obscurity 1.** the state or quality of being obscure.

discrepancy 1. the state or quality of being discrepant; <u>difference</u>; <u>inconsistency</u>. **hypocrisy 1.** a <u>pretense</u> of having a <u>virtuous</u> character, <u>moral</u> or <u>religious</u> beliefs or principles, and the like, that one does not really <u>possess</u>. **bane 1.** a person or thing that <u>ruins</u> or <u>spoils</u>.

Hidden Meanings Puzzle 6

myriad 1. a very <u>great</u> or <u>indefinitely</u> great <u>number</u> of persons or things. **deplete 1.** to <u>decrease</u> seriously or <u>exhaust</u> the <u>abundance</u> or supply of. **ambivalence 1.** uncertainty or <u>fluctuation</u>, especially when caused by <u>inability</u> to make a <u>choice</u> or by a <u>simultaneous</u> desire to say or do two opposite or <u>conflicting</u> things. **flourish 1.** to be in a <u>vigorous</u> state; <u>thrive</u>. **2.** to be in its or in one's <u>prime</u>; to be at the height of fame, <u>excellence</u>, influence, and so on. **3.** to be successful; <u>prosper</u>. **distend 1.** to make <u>larger</u> by stretching, as something hollow or <u>elastic</u>. **2.** to <u>spread</u> in all directions; expand; <u>swell</u>. **peripheral 1.** pertaining to, situated in, or constituting the <u>periphery</u>. **2.** concerned with relatively minor, <u>irrelevant</u>, or <u>superficial</u> aspects of the subject in question. **garner 1.** to gather or <u>deposit</u> in or as if in a granary or other <u>storage</u> place. **2.** to get; <u>acquire</u>; <u>earn</u>. **transient 1.** not lasting, <u>enduring</u>, or <u>permanent</u>; <u>transitory</u>. **2.** lasting only a <u>short</u> time; existing <u>briefly</u>; <u>temporary</u>. **virulent 1.** actively <u>poisonous</u>; intensely <u>noxious</u>. **2.** *Medical:* highly infective; <u>malignant</u> or deadly. **stymie 1.** a <u>situation</u> or problem presenting such <u>difficulties</u> as to discourage or <u>defeat</u> any attempt to deal with or <u>resolve</u> it.

Hidden Meanings Puzzle 7

fraudulent 1. characterized by, involving, or <u>proceeding</u> from <u>fraud</u>, as actions, <u>enterprise</u>, methods, or gains. **2.** given to or using fraud, as a person; <u>cheating</u>; <u>dishonest</u>. **obdurate 1.** <u>unmoved</u> by <u>persuasion</u>, pity, or tender feelings; stubborn; <u>unyielding</u>. **recalcitrant 1.** resisting <u>authority</u> or control; not obedient or <u>compliant</u>; <u>refractory</u>. **2.** <u>hard</u> to deal with, <u>manage</u>, or operate. **ephemeral 1.** lasting a <u>very</u> short time; short-lived; <u>transitory</u>. **salubrious 1.** <u>favorable</u> to or promoting health; healthful. **corroborate 1.** to make <u>certain</u>; to confirm. **munificent 1.** extremely <u>liberal</u> in <u>giving</u>; very <u>generous</u>. **parsimony 1.** extreme or <u>excessive</u> economy or frugality; <u>stinginess</u>. **surreptitious 1.** <u>obtained</u>, done, made, and so on by <u>stealth</u>; secret or <u>unauthorized</u>; <u>clandestine</u>. **dissonance 1.** <u>inharmonious</u> or harsh sound; <u>discord</u>; <u>cacophony</u>. **2.** *Music:* a simultaneous combination of tones conventionally accepted as being in a state of unrest and needing <u>completion</u>.

Hidden Meanings Puzzle 8

abstemious 1. sparing or <u>moderate</u> in eating and drinking; <u>temperate</u> in diet. **2.** characterized by <u>abstinence</u>. **subordinate 1.** placed in or <u>belonging</u> to a <u>lower</u> order or <u>rank</u>. **2.** of less importance; <u>secondary</u>. **3.** subject to or under the authority of a <u>superior</u>. **4.** <u>subservient</u> or inferior. **regress 1.** to move backwards; to go <u>back</u>. **2.** to <u>revert</u> to an earlier or less <u>advanced</u> state or form. **fractious 1.** <u>refractory</u> or unruly. **2.** readily angered; <u>peevish</u>; irritable; <u>quarrelsome</u>. **obsequious 1.** characterized by or showing <u>servile</u> complaisance or <u>deference</u>; <u>fawning</u>. **2.** servilely compliant or deferential. **emancipate 1.** to free from <u>restraint</u>, <u>influence</u>, or the like. **2.** to free (a slave) from <u>bondage</u>. **ingenuous 1.** free from reserve, restraint, or <u>dissimulation</u>; <u>candid</u>; sincere. **2.** artless; <u>innocent</u>; <u>naive</u>. **supercilious 1.** haughtily <u>disdainful</u> or contemptuous, as a person or a facial <u>expression</u>. **convivial 1.** <u>friendly</u>; agreeable. **2.** fond of <u>feasting</u>, drinking, and merry company; <u>jovial</u>. **3.** of or befitting a feast; <u>festive</u>. **coalesce 1.** to grow together or into one <u>body</u>. **2.** to <u>unite</u> so as to form one <u>mass</u>, community, and so forth.

CHAPTER 5 ANSWERS

Crossword Puzzle 7

Brainy People

Crossword Puzzle 8

Come on! Let's Get Going

Crossword Puzzle 9

P-U, That's Yucky!

Quotation Puzzle 3

Quote: Question: "What do you get when you don't pay your exorcist promptly? Answer: Repossessed." Unknown Author

Answers: **A.** STIMPY, **B.** SPURIOUS, **C.** TEXAS, **D.** TEETH, **E.** REDWOODS, **F.** WRONG, **G.** TOOLS, **H.** EQUATOR, **I.** DOPEY, **J.** PENURY, **K.** CHEWY, **L.** ANNOYS.

Quotation Puzzle 4

Quote: "With Congress, every time they make a joke it's a law. And every time they make a law it's a joke." Will Rogers

Answers: **A.** JOHN WOO, **B.** RICKI LAKE, **C.** VEHEMENT, **D.** ELIOT, **E.** HEAVY, **F.** TWEAK, **G.** MAJESTY, **H.** WALKS, **I.** SAILS, **J.** TEMERITY, **K.** GEYSER, **L.** EMIGRATE, **M.** AWARD.

Quotation Puzzle 5

Quote: "I never let my schooling interfere with my education." Mark Twain.

Answers: **A.** SHREWD, **B.** INGENUITY, **C.** THRIFTY, **D.** LACONIC, **E.** REVIEW, **F.** REMOTE, **G.** MAILMAN, **H.** TOKEN.

Cryptofamily Puzzle 5

ARCHAIC, HACKNEYED, OBSOLETE, SUPERANNUATE, OUTDATED, OLD-FASHIONED, PROTOTYPE, ANCESTRAL, ANTECEDENT, PROGENITOR, ORIGINAL, ANTIQUE, VINTAGE, OUTMODED.

Cryptofamily Puzzle 6

IRE, ENRAGE, INCENSE, PROVOKE, EXPLODE, FUME, RAGE, SEETHE, BRISTLE, BOIL, FURY, OUTRAGE, TORMENT, ANNOY.

Cryptofamily Puzzle 7

FOIL, FETTER, HAMPER, BAR, CONSTRAIN, CURB, CONFINE, CRAMP, STRICTURE, RESTRICT, SANCTION, FORBID, THWART, STYMIE.

Cryptofamily Puzzle 8

SANE, PRUDENT, LUCID, BALANCED, JUDICIOUS, REASONABLE, SAGACIOUS, SENSIBLE, WISE, PERCEPTIVE, COGNIZANT, DISCERNING, SAPIENT, COHERENT.

Cryptofamily Puzzle 9

WEAVE, WANDER, DEVIATE, ZIGZAG, SWERVE, TWIST, SNAKE, SKEW, SWAY, COIL, CORKSCREW, CURL, SPIRAL, TWINE.

Cryptofamily Puzzle 10

CRUEL, DEVILISH, GHOULISH, INFERNAL, OGREISH, SATANIC, BARBAROUS, BESTIAL, FERAL, FEROCIOUS, INHUMAN, SAVAGE, VICIOUS, WOLFISH.

Cryptofamily Puzzle 11

EXAGGERATE, HYPERBOLIZE, INFLATE, MAGNIFY, OVERCHARGE, OVERSTATE, AGGRANDIZE, ENNOBLE, SENSATIONALIZE, EMBELLISH, EMBROIDER, ENHANCE, AMPLIFY, VARNISH.

Cryptofamily Puzzle 12

PLEDGE, VOUCH FOR, PROMISE, AUTHENTICATE, SUBSTANTIATE, COMMIT, CORROBORATE, OBLIGATE, CERTIFY, VOW, CONTRACT, SWEAR, AVER, VERIFY.

Cryptofamily Puzzle 13

CAREFREE, DEBONAIR, SPRIGHTLY, LIGHTHEARTED, EXUBERANT, JOYFUL, EBULLIENT, EFFERVESCENT, VIVACIOUS, TRIUMPHANT, JUBILANT, EXULTATION, ANIMATED, VIGOROUS.

Cryptofamily Puzzle 14

BASE, COMMON, HUMBLE, IGNOBLE, ORDINARY, PLEBIAN, VULGAR, INFERIOR, MEDIOCRE, SHODDY, TRITE, CLICHÉ, BANAL, HACKNEYED.

Cryptofamily Puzzle 15

BEST, CONQUER, MASTER, PREVAIL, SURMOUNT, OVERCOME, TRIUMPH, DEFEAT, ROUT, SUBDUE, VANQUISH, TRANSCEND, EXCEED, SURPASS.

Cryptofamily Puzzle 16

EXTRAVAGANT, IMPROVIDENT, PRODIGAL, LAVISH, SPENDTHRIFT, EXCESS, GLUT, FAT, SUPERFLUOUS, SURPLUS, PROLIX, SURFEIT, IMMODERATE, REDUNDANT.

Groupie Puzzle 3

disintegrate, unravel, defective, languish, weaken, nonadhesion. Come apart at the seams.

Groupie Puzzle 4

finery, bejeweled, adorned, slay me, enchanting, sartorial elegance. Dressed to kill.

CHAPTER 6 ANSWERS

Crossword Puzzle 10

I Am So Sorry

Crossword Puzzle 11

He's the Quiet Type

Crossword Puzzle 12

Chill Pills

Word Creation Puzzle 2

dominant	attraction	proactive
dominate	extraction	inactive
indomitable	tractable	counteractive
dominator	intractable	reactive
matriarchy	tractate	react
anarchy	extractable	complicate
matriarch	attractable	implicate
cadence	excessive	explicate
incident	incessant	complicit
graduate	cede	revoke
digress	procession	vocation
digression	recess	provocation
stability	recession	provoke
instability	excess	invoke
stable	antecedent	invocation
instable	agent	provocate
attract	counteract	maternal
extract	inaction	

Word Creation Puzzle 3

sequel	credible	multifarious
consecutive	current	invention
mutation	cursory	convention
transmute	concurrent	prevention
immutable	facile	preventative
transmutation	factory	preventable
transmute	infection	convent
natal	fiction	inventory
native	defection	presume
nation	confection	consume
debase	defective	consumptive
basement	facilitate	consummate
incredible	convene	presumptive
credentials	multitude	summation

Word Creation Puzzle 4

acerbity	stricture	evacuate
acrimonious	stringent	vacation
audience	restrictor	revacate
auditory	omniscient	vacate
audible	intrude	vacuous
inaudible	intrusion	vaccine
docile	intruder	conscious
doctrine	protrusion	prescient
doctor	protrudence	science
document	vacant	philosopher

Word Creation Puzzle 5

biblical	submission	subscript
bibliography	admission	inscribe
chromatic	submit	prescribe
chronological	novelty	adapt
chronology	novice	convolution
chronograph	innovation	revolution
cosmic	prescription	devolution
dormant	description	revolve
dormitory	inscription	devolve
admit	subscription	graphology

Cryptofamily Puzzle 17

ACHE, AVARICIOUS, COVETOUS, DESIROUS, RAPACIOUS, ENVIOUS, GLUTTONOUS, GREEDY, CRAVE, HUNGER, YEARN, YEN, APPETITE, PASSIONATE.

Cryptofamily Puzzle 18

OMIT, SUBTRACT, DEDUCT, DIMINISH, CONDENSE, DECIMATE, EXCLUDE, EJECT, ALLEVIATE, ERADICATE, EXTIRPATE, EXPURGATE, OBLITERATE, ABRIDGE.

Cryptofamily Puzzle 19

FAIR, BEAUTEOUS, EXQUISITE, RADIANT, MAGNIFICENT, WINSOME, REFINED, ELEGANT, GLAMOROUS, CHIC, SUBLIME, RESPLENDENT, PULCHRITUDINOUS, STATUESQUE.

Cryptofamily Puzzle 20

ADAGE, MAXIM, PROVERB, APHORISM, EPIGRAM, MOTTO, SLOGAN, EPITHET, AXIOM, TRUISM, BANALITY, CLICHE, BROMIDE, DICTUM.

Cryptofamily Puzzle 21

DISSIDENT, NONCONFORMIST, PROTESTANT, SECTARIAN, PARTISAN, SEPARATIST, SCHISMATIC, MALCONTENT, DETRACTOR, CONSCIENTIOUS OBJECTOR, UNCONVENTIONALIST, BOHEMIAN, DISSENTIENT, FACTIONALIST.

Cryptofamily Puzzle 22

SCAN, MONITOR, SURVEY, SCRUTINIZE, RECONNOITER, SCOUT, PERUSE, GAPE, GAWK, OGLE, READ, INVIGILATE, SPECTATE, WITNESS.

Cryptofamily Puzzle 23

EFFUSIVE, INTENSE, IMPASSIONED, ZEALOUS, VEHEMENT, PASSIONATE, RAPTUROUS, ECSTATIC, INFLAMED, IMPETUOUS, TEMPERAMENTAL, VOLATILE, MELODRAMATIC, FANATICAL.

Cryptofamily Puzzle 24

GRANDILOQUENT, RHETORICAL, IMPERIOUS, ERUDITE, ORATORY, ELOQUENCE, DIDACTIC, CONVOLUTED, PROFOUND, DOGMATIC, SAGACIOUS, INDOCTRINATE, ESOTERIC, ARCANE.

Cryptofamily Puzzle 25

AFFABLE, GENIAL, AVUNCULAR, CORDIAL, COURTEOUS, CONGENIAL, BLITHE, PHILANTHROPIC, BENIGN, WINSOME, AMIABLE, FELICITOUS, SANGUINE, JOCULAR.

Cryptofamily Puzzle 26

QUERULOUS, ALOOF, DISCORDANT, CANTANKEROUS, ABRASIVE, BRUSQUE, MALEVOLENT, PERNICIOUS, NEFARIOUS, CONTEMPTUOUS, COMBATIVE, INCORRIGIBLE, FRACTIOUS, HAUGHTY.

Cryptofamily Puzzle 27

AGITATE, ENGENDER, TANTALIZE, CAJOLE, INCITE, PROVOKE, ACTIVATE, PROD, COERCE, GOAD, CONSCRIPT, IGNITE, ENJOIN, AROUSE.

Cryptofamily Puzzle 28

CHIDE, EXCORIATE, DISRESPECT, CHASTISE, DENIGRATE, DISPARAGE, LAMBASTE, REPRIMAND, CENSURE, REPROACH, MALIGN, VILIFY, BELITTLE, BERATE.

Phobia Puzzle 2

1. m, **2.** t, **3.** b, **4.** i, **5.** p, **6.** a, **7.** n, **8.** d, **9.** r, **10.** v, **11.** g, **12.** z, **13.** e, **14.** y, **15.** f, **16.** k, **17.** x, **18.** j, **19.** h, **20.** l, **21.** w, **22.** u, **23.** o, **24.** s, **25.** c, **26.** q.

Phobia Puzzle 3

1. v, **2.** p, **3.** h, **4.** z, **5.** b, **6.** s, **7.** m, **8.** l, **9.** a, **10.** f, **11.** y, **12.** r, **13.** e, **14.** u, **15.** c, **16.** x, **17.** j, **18.** d, **19.** w, **20.** k, **21.** g, **22.** o, **23.** i, **24.** n, **25.** q, **25.** t.

CHAPTER 7 ANSWERS

Quotation Puzzle 6

Quote: *"If you can't annoy somebody with what you write, I think there's little point in writing."*
Kingsley Amis. Acrostic: About Writing

Answers: **A.** ANIMOSITY, **B.** BROWN, **C.** OKLAHOMA, **D.** UNIFY, **E.** TWITCHY, **F.** WHITE HOUSE, **G.** ROYALTY, **H.** INSIPID, **I.** TWINGES, **J.** INTENT, **K.** NIKE, **L.** GLITTER.

Quotation Puzzle 7

Quote: *"A man walks into a psychiatrist's office with a banana up his nose and says, 'What's the matter with me, Doc?' The psychiatrist says, 'You're not eating properly.'" Acrostic: Truly Lame Yet Funny.*

Answers: **A.** THE ROCK, **B.** RASPS, **C.** USHER, **D.** LAFITTE, **E.** YOSHI, **F.** LABYRINTH, **G.** APT TO, **H.** MATHEMATICS, **I.** EAST ASIA, **J.** YO-YOS, **K.** EINSTEIN, **L.** THROWAWAY, **M.** FANATICISM, **N.** UP-AND-DOWN, **O.** NIGHTS, **P.** NEWSPAPER, **Q.** YACHTS.

Quotation Puzzle 8

Quote: *"As long as we live in a democracy, there is one basic truth that gives me hope. The chairman of Exxon has the same number of votes as you or I—one." Acrostic: Michael Moore Opinion*

Answers: **A.** MARIAH CAREY, **B.** IGLOOS, **C.** CHEFS, **D.** HEMS, **E.** ABATE, **F.** EXHAUSTIVE, **G.** LEAVES, **H.** MOTHS, **I.** OVENS, **J.** OMENS, **K.** ROUGH, **L.** EXTRICATES, **M.** ORNATE, **N.** PHONE, **O.** IOWA, **P.** NEMO, **Q.** INCH, **R.** OBDURATE, **S.** NIFTY.

Anagram Magic Square Puzzle 7

1. Thaws, **2.** Rogue, **3.** Ulcer, **4.** Navel, **5.** Cadge, **6.** Alloy, **7.** Trips, **8.** Equip, **9.** Denim.
SAT Word: Truncated.

Anagram Magic Square Puzzle 8

1. Nerve, **2.** Organ, **3.** Throb, **4.** Odors, **5.** Rider, **6.** Idles, **7.** Ovals, **8.** Upset, **9.** Sprig.
SAT Word: Notorious.

Anagram Magic Square Puzzle 9

1. Wrong, **2.** Heaps, **3.** Idyll, **4.** Mares, **5.** Study, **6.** Idols, **7.** Coins, **8.** Amber, **9.** Lever.
SAT Word: Whimsical.

Crossword Puzzle 13

L	A	M	P	S		R	T	S		A	D	D	L	E
A	W	A	I	T		E	A	U		T	R	U	E	S
D	E	C	E	I	T	F	U	L		T	U	B	E	S
		L	I	E		F	U	N	G	I				
T	R	A	I	T	O	R	O	U	S		S	O	U	L
K	I	L	N	S		E	R	R	O	R		U	S	A
O	M	I	T		L	E	G		P	U	R	S	E	S
		R	E	A	D		P	E	T	A				
I	N	F	A	M	Y		B	E	N		B	R	E	D
C	P	U		S	U	S	A	N		A	B	O	D	E
E	R	R	S		P	E	R	N	I	C	I	O	U	S
		T	U	L	S	A		A	N	T				
A	M	I	G	O		C	O	N	N	I	V	I	N	G
N	O	V	A	S		O	R	T		V	I	N	C	I
D	E	E	R	S		W	E	S		E	N	D	O	N

Sneaky People

Crossword Puzzle 14

A	B	S		A	C	E		H	I	P	N	E	S	S
C	E	E		R	A	N		E	N	L	A	R	G	E
C	A	R	P	E	R	S		A	C	E	T	A	T	E
O	V	E	R	A	B	U	N	D	A	N	T			
R	E	N	E		S	E	A		T	Y	P	E	S	
D	R	E	A	M		S	U	D	S	Y		A	L	L
		M	A	T		T	O	P		C	H	O		
S	U	R	P	L	U	S		S	U	R	F	E	I	T
I	R	A		B	A	D		R	O	O				
P	S	I		P	A	L	E	D		D	R	E	S	S
S	A	L	S	A		M	E	D		M	I	L	A	
		P	R	O	L	I	F	E	R	A	T	E	S	
B	E	R	E	A	V	E		C	L	O	T	H	E	S
A	R	C	A	D	E	S		O	A	T		E	V	E
T	E	A	R	E	R	S		N	Y	C		R	E	D

Too Much, Man

Crossword Puzzle 15

D	O	W	N		G	R	I	M	M		D	R	A	G
E	R	I	C		M	A	N	I	A		I	O	W	A
M	E	L	A	N	C	H	O	L	Y		S	L	E	D
I	O	T	A	S		R	E	A		M	E	S	S	
			A	G	E	D		S	T	A				
H	A	V	E		E	X	E	S		O	L	S	E	N
I	R	A	N		T	A	R	I	F	F		A	L	I
D	O	L	E	F	U	L		M	A	U	D	L	I	N
E	M	O		O	P	T	S	I	N		A	S	E	A
F	A	R	S	I		S	W	A	N		M	A	S	S
		O	L	D		A	N	Y	A					
R	E	A	L		O	R	G		I	M	P	L	Y	
U	R	G	E		L	U	G	U	B	R	I	O	U	S
G	L	U	M		O	B	E	S	E		C	U	R	L
S	E	E	N		R	E	R	A	N		A	R	E	S

Bummed Out

Crossword Puzzle 16

N	O	V		O	P	T	T	O		S	C	A	M
O	U	I		W	A	R	H	O	L		I	O	W	A
G	R	E	G	A	R	I	O	U	S		A	R	E	S
		T	A	C		C	U	R	E		M	D	S	
W	I	N	S	O	M	E		E	N	S		I	O	N
T	R	A	P		A	T	A	D		W	H	A	M	O
S	A	M		L	I	A	M		H	E	A	L	E	D
		C	O	N	G	E	N	I	A	L				
G	I	J	A	N	E		B	E	R	T		C	I	A
A	M	O	N	G		S	A	G	A		W	A	L	L
B	I	C		S	A	P		A	M	I	A	B	L	E
	T	U	T		S	E	C	T		R	I	O		
M	A	L	I		F	E	L	I	C	I	T	O	U	S
E	T	A	L		O	D	I	O	U	S		S	P	A
G	E	R	E		R	O	O	N	E		E	C	O	

Affable People

Hidden Meanings Puzzle 9

intransigent **1.** refusing to agree or <u>compromise</u>; <u>uncompromising</u>; <u>inflexible</u>. **cogent** **1.** convincing or <u>believable</u> by virtue of <u>forceful</u>, clear, or <u>incisive</u> presentation; telling. **2.** to the point; <u>relevant</u>; <u>pertinent</u>. **redundant** **1.** characterized by <u>verbosity</u> or unnecessary <u>repetition</u> in expressing ideas; <u>prolix</u>. **humdrum** **1.** <u>lacking</u> variety; boring; <u>dull</u>. **2.** tedious character or <u>routine</u>; <u>monotony</u>.

prodigal 1. wastefully or <u>recklessly</u> <u>extravagant</u>. **2.** giving or yielding <u>profusely</u>; <u>lavish</u>. **impudent 1.** of, pertaining to, or characterized by <u>impertinence</u> or <u>effrontery</u>. **loquacious 1.** talking or tending to talk much or freely; <u>talkative</u>; <u>chattering</u>; babbling; <u>garrulous</u>. **2.** characterized by <u>excessive</u> talk; <u>wordy</u>. **consensus 1.** <u>majority</u> of <u>opinion</u>. **2.** general agreement or <u>concord</u>; <u>harmony</u>. **ignominy 1.** <u>disgrace</u>; dishonor; public <u>contempt</u>. **2.** <u>shameful</u> or dishonorable quality or <u>conduct</u> or an instance of this. **malign 1.** to speak <u>harmful</u> untruths about; speak <u>evil</u> of; <u>slander</u>; <u>defame</u>. **2.** evil in effect; <u>pernicious</u>; baleful; <u>injurious</u>.

Hidden Meanings Puzzle 10

aberration 1. the act of departing from the <u>right</u>, normal, or usual <u>course</u>. **2.** the act of <u>deviating</u> from the <u>ordinary</u>, usual, or normal type. **insidious 1.** intended to <u>entrap</u> or <u>beguile</u>. **2.** stealthily <u>treacherous</u> or deceitful. **3.** operating or proceeding in an <u>inconspicuous</u> or seemingly harmless way but actually with <u>grave</u> effect. **juxtapose 1.** to place close <u>together</u> or side by side, especially for <u>comparison</u> or <u>contrast</u>. **jocular 1.** given to, characterized by, intended for, or suited to joking or <u>jesting</u>; waggish; <u>facetious</u>. **interminable 1.** incapable of being <u>terminated</u>; <u>unending</u>. **2.** <u>monotonously</u> or annoyingly <u>protracted</u> or continued; unceasing; <u>incessant</u>. **laggard 1.** a person or thing that lags; <u>lingerer</u>; <u>loiterer</u>. **2.** moving, developing, or responding slowly; <u>sluggish</u>; <u>dilatory</u>; backward. **prone 1.** having a natural <u>inclination</u> or tendency to something; <u>disposed</u>; <u>liable</u>. **2.** having the front or <u>ventral</u> part downward; <u>lying</u> face downward. **trite 1.** lacking in freshness or <u>effectiveness</u> because of constant use or <u>excessive</u> repetition; <u>hackneyed</u>. **volition 1.** the act of willing, choosing, or <u>resolving</u>. **2.** a choice or <u>decision</u> made by the will. **untenable 1.** <u>incapable</u> of being <u>defended</u>, as an argument, thesis, and so on; <u>indefensible</u>. **2.** not fit to be <u>occupied</u>, as an apartment, house, and the like.

Hidden Meanings Puzzle 11

amalgamate 1. to mix or <u>merge</u> so as to make a <u>combination</u>; blend; unite; combine. **2.** to combine, unite, merge, or <u>coalesce</u>. **cloistered 1.** <u>secluded</u> from the world; <u>sheltered</u>. **talisman 1.** a stone, ring, or other object, engraved with figures or <u>characters</u> supposed to possess <u>occult</u> powers and worn as an <u>amulet</u> or charm. **inanimate 1.** not animate; <u>lifeless</u>. **2.** spiritless; <u>sluggish</u>; <u>dull</u>. **perplexity 1.** the state of being perplexed; <u>confusion</u>; <u>uncertainty</u>. **2.** a <u>tangled</u>, involved, or confused condition or <u>situation</u>. **enigma 1.** a puzzling or <u>inexplicable</u> occurrence or situation. **2.** a person of puzzling or <u>contradictory</u> character. **3.** a saying, question, picture, and the like containing a <u>hidden</u> meaning; <u>riddle</u>. **crass 1.** without <u>refinement</u>, delicacy, or <u>sensitivity</u>; gross; <u>obtuse</u>; stupid. **fortuitous 1.** <u>happening</u> or produced by <u>chance</u>; <u>accidental</u>. **2.** <u>lucky</u>; <u>fortunate</u>. **preposterous 1.** completely <u>contrary</u> to nature, <u>reason</u>, or common sense; <u>absurd</u>; senseless; utterly <u>foolish</u>. **squalid 1.** foul and <u>repulsive</u>, as from lack of care or cleanliness; <u>neglected</u> and <u>filthy</u>. **2.** wretched; miserable; <u>degraded</u>; sordid.

Hidden Meanings Puzzle 12

uproarious 1. characterized by or in a state of uproar; <u>tumultuous</u>. **2.** making an uproar; <u>confused</u> and <u>noisy</u>, as an assembly, person, and so on. **winsome 1.** sweetly or <u>innocently</u> charming; <u>winning</u>; <u>engaging</u>. **plunder 1.** to rob of goods or <u>valuables</u> by open <u>force</u>, as in war, <u>hostile</u> raids, <u>brigandage</u>, and so forth. **2.** to rob, despoil, or <u>fleece</u>. **3.** to take wrongfully, as by <u>pillage</u>, robbery, or <u>fraud</u>. **harrowing 1.** extremely <u>disturbing</u> or distressing; <u>grievous</u>. **gargantuan 1.** <u>gigantic</u>; <u>enormous</u>;

colossal. **churlish 1.** like a churl; <u>boorish</u>; rude. **2.** of a churl; <u>peasantlike</u>. **wheedle 1.** to <u>endeavor</u> to influence (a person) by smooth, <u>flattering</u>, or <u>beguiling</u> words or acts. **fallacious 1.** containing a <u>fallacy</u>; logically <u>unsound</u>. **2.** <u>deceptive</u>; misleading. **congeal 1.** to change from a soft or <u>fluid</u> state to a <u>rigid</u> or solid state, as by cooling or <u>freezing</u>. **2.** to curdle; <u>coagulate</u>, as a fluid. **fiasco 1.** a complete and <u>ignominious</u> <u>failure</u>.

Hidden Meanings Puzzle 13

wraith 1. an <u>apparition</u> of a living person supposed to <u>portend</u> his or her death. **2.** a <u>visible</u> <u>spirit</u>. **propinquity 1.** nearness in place; <u>proximity</u>. **2.** nearness of relation; <u>kinship</u>. **3.** <u>affinity</u> of nature; <u>similarity</u>. **epitaph 1.** a commemorative <u>inscription</u> on a <u>tomb</u> or <u>mortuary</u> monument about the person buried at that site. **2.** a brief <u>poem</u> or other writing in praise of a <u>deceased</u> person. **abyss 1.** a deep, <u>immeasurable</u> space, gulf, or <u>cavity</u>; <u>vast</u> chasm. **2.** anything <u>profound</u>, <u>unfathomable</u>, or <u>infinite</u>. **paragon 1.** a model or <u>pattern</u> of <u>excellence</u> or of a <u>particular</u> excellence. **visceral 1.** of or pertaining to the <u>viscera</u>. **2.** characterized by or proceeding from <u>instinct</u> rather than <u>intellect</u>. **3.** characterized by or dealing with <u>coarse</u> or base emotions; <u>earthy</u>. **perspicacity 1.** <u>keenness</u> of mental <u>perception</u> and understanding; <u>discernment</u>; <u>penetration</u>. **decipher 1.** to make out the <u>meaning</u> of [poor or partially <u>obliterated</u> writing, etc.]. **2.** to discover the meaning of [anything <u>obscure</u> or difficult to <u>trace</u> or <u>understand</u>]. **facade 1.** *Architecture:* the <u>front</u> of a building, especially an <u>imposing</u> or <u>decorative</u> one. **2.** a <u>superficial</u> appearance or <u>illusion</u> of something. **prurient 1.** having, inclined to have, or characterized by <u>lascivious</u> or <u>lustful</u> thoughts, <u>desires</u>, and the like.

CHAPTER 8 ANSWERS

Crossword Puzzle 17

L	U	N	A	R		D	I	P	S		M	A	C	E
A	M	I	L	E		E	V	I	L		I	B	E	T
C	A	P	I	T	U	L	A	T	E		N	O	A	H
		B	I	L	L	N	Y	E		U	R	S	A	
R	E	C	A	N	T			K	I	T	T	E	N	
A	M	E	B	A		C	A	D		N	E	S	S	
G	I	L	A		D	E	S	I	S	T				
E	L	L		C	U	R	T	A	I	L		B	U	D
		H	O	T	E	L	S		T	I	R	E	
	C	H	O	U		S	R	S		T	I	N	G	E
D	H	A	R	M	A			H	I	N	D	E	R
A	I	R	S		U	N	R	E	A	D	Y		
U	N	D	O		D	E	B	I	L	I	T	A	T	E
N	O	U	N		E	R	I	N		E	I	D	E	R
T	S	P	S		N	O	S	E		S	M	E	A	R

Enough Already. I Give Up.

Crossword Puzzle 18

C	A	R		B	L	O	N	D	E		I	V	A	N
A	G	E		R	O	W	E	R	S		M	E	S	A
L	O	Q	U	A	C	I	O	U	S		P	R	A	Y
	U	P	T	O	N			D	E	B		
C	R	I	B	S		G	A	R	R	U	L	O	U	S
B	A	R	E		T	R	Y	O	N		S	P	A
S	H	E	A		H	O	T	E	L	S		E	S	P
	T	O	Y			E	T	C		
L	I	V		N	A	P	L	E	S		A	W	E	S
E	M	O		E	T	H	E	L			R	I	L	E
T	A	L	K	A	T	I	V	E		G	E	N	I	E
	U	R	L			G	A	L	E	S		
A	M	B	I		V	O	C	I	F	E	R	O	U	S
R	O	L	L		I	N	T	E	R	N		U	S	A
K	E	E	L		P	E	R	S	O	N		T	E	D

Will You Please Be Quiet!

Crossword Puzzle 19

Gimme More!

Groupie Puzzle 5

melodious, symphonic, supplanting, proxy, party game, lounge. Musical chairs.

Groupie Puzzle 6

assume, misinterpret, err, hypothesize, speculate, faulty logic. Get the wrong idea.

Groupie Puzzle 7

linchpin, anchor, converge, essence, pivotal, substance. Crux of the matter.

Groupie Puzzle 8

mandatory, postal worker's oath, tenacious, precipitation, solar, inclement. Come rain or shine.

Groupie Puzzle 9

shrewd, fallacious, duplicity, biased, obscured, facade. Hidden agenda.

Groupie Puzzle 10

conceited, haughty, reflector, exquisite, superlative, gorgeous. Mirror, mirror, on the wall.

Groupie Puzzle 11

exasperate, harass, exile, structure, incline, dominate. Drive up the wall.

Groupie Puzzle 12

meander, obfuscate, stymie, perplex, equivocate, waltz. Dance around the issue.

Groupie Puzzle 13

vanity, Ponce de Leon, fantasy, utopian, maturation, pubescence. Fountain of youth.

Cryptofamily Puzzle 29

CANTANKEROUS, CRANKY, OBSTINATE, VEXING, QUERULOUS, PERVERSE, PEEVISH, IRASCIBLE, CONTENTIOUS, CHURLISH, CALLOUS, ANNOYING, PETULANT, ORNERY.

Cryptofamily Puzzle 30

RARITY, MARVEL, MIRACLE, EXCEPTION, PHENOMENON, WONDER, SURPRISE, SHOCK, PRODIGY, ENIGMA, CURIOSITY, ODDITY, PARAGON, MASTERPIECE.

Cryptofamily Puzzle 31

CLAUSE, INGREDIENT, FRAGMENT, FRACTION, CATEGORY, ALLOTMENT, BRANCH, MORSEL, ELEMENT, DIVISION, DEPARTMENT, PORTION, DETRITUS, COMPONENT.

Cryptofamily Puzzle 32

UNBIND, LIBERATE, UNSHACKLE, DEREGULATE, EXTRICATE, PAROLE, UNLEASH, RELEASE, DISCHARGE, ACQUIT, RESCUE, REDEEM, REPRIEVE, DELIVER.

Cryptofamily Puzzle 33

PRECURSOR, HARBINGER, FOREWORD, PROLOGUE, PREMONITION, PREQUEL, VANGUARD, PREEMPTION, ANTECEDENCE, PRELUDE, OVERTURE, PREDICTION, TRAILBLAZER, TRENDSETTER.

Cryptofamily Puzzle 34

COVERT, HIBERNATING, INVISIBLE, SEQUESTERED, SUBCONSCIOUS, DORMANT, LATENT, QUIESCENT, IMPENETRABLE, OBSCURE, SECLUDED, SUBLIMINAL, UNMANIFESTED, LURKING.

Cryptofamily Puzzle 35

IMPEL, PROPAGATE, SIRE, COMPEL, FOMENT, PRECIPITATE, INAUGURATE, INSTIGATE, BROACH, FOSTER, KINDLE, BEGET, CULTIVATE, TEMPT.

Cryptofamily Puzzle 36

CALM, INDESTRUCTIBLE, STEADFAST, DURABLE, IRREVERSIBLE, INFLEXIBLE, ENTRENCHED, IMPERTURBABLE, IMMUTABLE, INEXTINGUISHABLE, PERPETUAL, PERENNIAL, INDELIBLE, BALANCED.

Cryptofamily Puzzle 37

DIGEST, ABBREVIATION, SUMMARY, SYNOPSIS, SURVEY, ABSTRACT, OUTLINE, SKETCH, DIAGRAM, DELINEATION, CONDENSATION, CONTRACTION, SILHOUETTE, CONTOUR.

Cryptofamily Puzzle 38

GILDED, OSTENTATIOUS, GAUDY, EXTRAVAGANT, HYPERBOLIC, BEJEWELED, EMBELLISHED, DECORATIVE, ORNATE, AFFECTED, POMPOUS, GRANDIOSE, ADORNED, ENHANCED.

Cryptofamily Puzzle 39

GENIAL, COMPANIONABLE, URBANE, AMIABLE, GREGARIOUS, EXTROVERTED, JOVIAL, CORDIAL, COMMUNICATIVE, AMICABLE, SOCIABLE, CHARISMATIC, CONVIVIAL, OUTGOING.

Cryptofamily Puzzle 40

DIN, REVERBERATION, CACHINNATION, CLANGOR, CRESCENDO, FANFARE, TUMULT, VOCIFERATION, ULULATION, BEDLAM, PANDEMONIUM, TURMOIL, BOMBARDMENT, CLAMOR.

Cryptofamily Puzzle 41

FATAL, DECEASED, DEMISED, BREATHLESS, MORIBUND, PERISHING, EXTINCT, LETHAL, TERMINAL, CADAVEROUS, LIVID, PALLID, DEFUNCT, LIFELESS.

Cryptofamily Puzzle 42

DANTE & BEATRICE, ANTONY & CLEOPATRA, EROS & PSYCHE, GERTRUDE STEIN & ALICE B. TOKLAS, JANE EYRE & EDWARD ROCHESTER, PARIS & HELEN, HEATHCLIFF & CATHY, CAROLYN BESSETTE & JOHN KENNEDY, ROMEO & JULIET, ANNA KARENINA & ALEKSEI VRONSKI, NAPOLEON & JOSEPHINE, SCARLETT O'HARA & RHETT BUTLER, LANCELOT & GUINEVERE, SONNY & CHER, DAVID & BATHSHEBA, LADY DIANA & PRINCE CHARLES.

CHAPTER 9 ANSWERS

Crossword Puzzle 20

A Vocabulary Builder

Anagram Magic Square Puzzle 10

1. Earthy, **2.** Patrol, **3.** Hounds, **4.** Editor, **5.** Meteor, **6.** Endows, **7.** Racoon, **8.** Airman, **9.** Lovely.
SAT Word: Ephemeral.

Anagram Magic Square Puzzle 11

1. Cliche, **2.** Obsess, **3.** Napped, **4.** Unreal, **5.** Nearer, **6.** Dasher, **7.** Ringer, **8.** Unfelt, **9.** Meaner.
SAT Word: Conundrum.

Word within Word Puzzle 4

ANTHROPOCENTRISM—16 letters

aces	airmen	anterior
acetic	airs	anthem
achromic	amen	anthropic
acorn	amine	ante
acre	amino	antic
action	anchor	antiphon
actor	ancient	aortic
acts	anoint	aphorism
aims	another	apricot

apron	case	crop
apse	cast	each
arch	caste	east
arise	cater	eats
armoire	cent	enact
armor	chair	entropic
armpit	chant	errant
armrest	chase	hair
arrest	chaste	hamper
arsenic	chime	hamster
arson	chimp	hansom
arthroscope	chin	hare
arts	chip	harem
ascent	chirp	harm
ascot	choose	harmonic
ashen	chop	harp
ashore	chore	harpoon
aspect	chose	hart
aspen	chrome	hasp
aspic	coat	haste
aspire	coins	hatch
aster	cone	hate
astern	coop	hatter
astir	cooper	heart
astronomer	cope	heat
atheism	core	hector
atom	corn	hemp
attic	cornet	hems
came	corset	henna
camper	cosine	hernia
cane	cosmos	hero
canine	cost	heroin
cape	crest	heroism
caret	crime	heron
carpet	crimp	hers
carrot	croon	hire
cart	crooner	hoarse

home	match	mother
hone	mate	motor
hoop	matron	name
horn	matter	nape
horse	mean	nectar
hose	meat	nomic
host	meet	nonatomic
hotter	mention	none
import	merchant	nonhero
important	merit	noon
inane	mesh	norm
income	mete	nose
intact	meter	oats
ions	metric	ocean
iota	mice	ointment
irons	mince	omen
mace	miner	omnipotent
machine	minor	onset
macho	mint	open
main	mire	opera
mane	miscreant	operation
manioc	miser	other
manner	mist	otter
manor	mite	pace
mansion	mitten	pain
maps	mocha	paint
march	moiré	pair
mare	moist	pane
marine	monarch	panic
maroon	monastic	pant
marsh	monitor	pantheon
marten	monster	panther
martin	month	pants
mash	moon	parish
mason	moose	pare
mast	more	parse
master	most	part

paste	print	room
patch	prior	roost
pate	prison	root
path	prominent	rope
patriot	promise	roster
patter	prone	rotate
pear	prose	rotor
penchant	race	rotten
pension	rain	saint
person	raise	same
pert	ramp	sanction
pest	ransom	sapient
pesto	rant	sari
phase	rape	satin
phone	rapt	scam
phonetic	rare	scamper
phrase	rasp	scan
picot	ratchet	scant
pier	rate	scar
pincer	rather	scare
pins	ratio	scat
pint	ration	scathe
pitcher	reach	scatter
pittance	remain	scent
poem	reap	schema
poor	remit	schmo
pore	repair	scion
port	repast	scone
porter	report	scoop
pose	resin	scope
post	rich	score
poster	riot	scorpion
praise	ripe	scram
preach	risen	scrap
price	roam	scrape
primate	roast	scrimp
prince	romper	scrip

script	smart	spire
seam	smear	spit
search	smirch	spite
seat	smooth	spoon
secant	smother	spore
section	snap	sport
semipro	snip	spot
senator	snitch	sprint
senior	snoop	stain
sent	snoot	stair
sepia	snore	stamen
septic	soap	stamp
sermon	soar	star
shame	sociopath	starch
shampoo	some	stare
shape	sonic	start
share	sonnet	state
sharp	soon	static
shear	soot	steam
shim	soothe	stem
shin	sore	stench
shine	sort	step
ship	sortie	stern
shirt	space	stint
shoe	spam	stir
shoot	span	stitch
shop	spar	stoic
shore	spare	stomach
short	spat	stomp
shrimp	spatter	stone
sierra	spear	stoop
simper	spent	stop
since	sperm	store
sine	sphincter	storm
siphon	spice	strain
sire	spin	strait
siren	spine	strap

stream

stretch

strict

strip

stripe

tacit

tact

taint

tame

tanner

tape

taste

teach

team

teapot

tear

teaspoon

tempo

tempt

tenant

tenor

tension

tensor

tent

term

terminator

test

than

that

thematic

theorist

thin

this

thorn

those

threat

thrice

throe

throne

tier

time

tint

tips

tiptoe

tires

tithe

toaster

torne

tone

toot

tooth

topic

topper

tops

torch

torment

torso

tort

torte

tortoise

totem

traces

tract

train

trait

traitor

tramp

trance

transcript

transient

transit

transmit

transpire

trap

trash

treason

treat

tremor

trench

triceps

tricorn

tricot

trim

trio

trip

trite

tropics

tropism

trot

tsar

561 words

Word within Word Puzzle 5

CIRCUMLOCUTIONS—15 letters

circuitous

circus

citron

clinic

clot

clout

coco

coconut

coil

coin

colic

colitis

colon

column

color

comic

conic

control

concur

consort

consul

contour

corn

cortisol

cosmic

cost

council

count

cousin

crust

cult

icon

ilium

incisor

incult

incur

inmost

insult

into

intro

iron

ions

isotonic

licit

limit

lint

lion

list

litmus

loco

locus

locution

loin

loom

loon

loot

loris

lorn

lost

lots

lotus

lout

micro

minor

minus

miscount

miso

mist

moist

molt

monitor

moon

moor

moot

morn

moron

most

motion

motor

moult

mount

mourn

mouton

mucous

mucus

multicolor

music

must

mutinous

nitric

nitrous

norm

nostrum

nuts

occult

oculist

oils

olio

omit

onto

onus

ours

oust

outs

outrun

rims

riot

room

root

rosin

rostrum

roust

rout

ruin

runt

rust

silicon

silt

sitcom

slim

slit

slot

slum

smolt

smut

snit

snort	stimulus	torn
snoot	stir	torsion
snout	stoic	torso
soil	stool	tour
solicit	storm	tourism
solo	strum	tricolor
solution	stucco	tricot
sonic	succor	trim
soon	suction	trio
soot	surmount	tumor
sort	tocsin	tunic
soul	soil	turmoil
sour	tonic	turn
stern	tool	

167 words

Word within Word Puzzle 6

DISINGENUOUS—12 letters

deign	guise	sing
design	guns	sinuous
digs	ingenuous	sinus
dine	inside	sinusoid
dingo	neon	snide
disguise	nine	snug
disunion	node	song
done	noise	sound
dose	none	souse
douse	nose	suds
dune	nude	sued
dung	nudge	suns
ensign	odes	undone
genius	ones	unsound
gods	send	unused
gone	side	using
guess	sign	
guide	sine	

52 words

Word within Word Puzzle 7

EQUIVOCATE—10 letters

acquit	cute	quite
active	equate	quota
auto	evict	quote
cave	give	toque
cite	iota	veto
coat	octave	vice
coquet	ovate	voice
cove	quiet	vote
covet	quit	

26 words

Word within Word Puzzle 8

LOQUACIOUS—10 letters

ails	loco	quasi
also	locus	sail
coal	oils	social
coil	olio	soil
cola	oscula	soul
loci	quail	usual

18 words

Word within Word Puzzle 9

MACHINATIONS—12 letters

action	atomic	cats
aims	atonic	chain
amino	caiman	chamois
animation	cannot	chant
amnion	canon	chaos
anoint	cant	chasm
anon	cantina	chat
antic	canto	chin
ants	cash	china
ascot	casino	chino
asthma	cast	chit

coast	mast	scant
coats	mastic	scat
coma	match	schmo
contain	mats	sham
cost	mica	shim
cots	minion	shin
hansom	mint	shot
hint	moan	simian
hoist	moat	sitcom
host	moist	smith
hosanna	month	snatch
icon	mosaic	snit
inaction	moth	snot
inch	nacho	somatic
into	nation	sonata
itch	niacin	sonic
mach	ninth	stain
machinist	nits	stamina
main	notch	stanch
maintain	oath	stoic
manla	oats	stoma
maniac	omit	stomach
manioc	saint	tahini
mannish	sanction	than
mantis	satanic	thin
mascot	satin	this
mash	scam	tonic
mason	scan	

116 words

Quotation Puzzle 9

Quote: "Every decade thinks its clothing styles have substance. But remember: One era's ultimate fashion statement will someday be another era's silly Halloween costume." Acrostic: Dennis Miller Rants.

Answers: **A.** DUMBO, **B.** EMILY WATSON, **C.** NEFARIOUS, **D.** NICK LACHEY, **E.** IMMUNE, **F.** SHUTTLES, **G.** MELANCHOLY, **H.** ITALY, **I.** LATEST, **J.** LET IT BE, **K.** ENGENDERS, **L.** ROBERT E. LEE, **M.** RAVES, **N.** ABRASIVE, **O.** NEWSCASTS, **P.** THE THAMES, **Q.** SOOTHED.

Quotation Puzzle 10

Quote: "Do you know the difference between 'village' and 'hamlet'? Surprisingly few people do, but it's quite simple really: one is a place where people live and the other is a play by Shakespeare."
Acrostic: Bill Bryson, Easy English

Answers: **A.** BOB HOPE, **B.** IMPUDENCE, **C.** LIPTON, **D.** LATERAL, **E.** BUFFALO, **F.** RON HOWARD, **G.** YEAST, **H.** SWEEPS WEEK, **I.** OLIVE, **J.** NEPHEW, **K.** ERUDITE, **L.** ANTIPATHY, **M.** SQUEAL, **N.** YELLS, **O.** EMPLOY, **P.** NEEDLE, **Q.** GRATIFY, **R.** LEASE, **S.** INCISIVE, **T.** SKIPPER, **U.** HEATH LEDGER.

Hidden Meanings Puzzle 14

archaic 1. <u>marked</u> by the <u>characteristics</u> of an <u>earlier period</u>; <u>antiquated</u>. **edify 1.** to <u>instruct</u> or <u>benefit</u>, especially <u>morally</u> or <u>spiritually</u>; <u>uplift</u>. **gregarious 1.** <u>fond</u> of the <u>company</u> of <u>others</u>; <u>sociable</u>. **pejorative 1.** having a <u>disparaging</u>, <u>derogatory</u>, or <u>belittling</u> <u>effect</u> or <u>force</u>. **vernacular 1.** (of language) <u>native</u> or <u>indigenous</u> (as <u>opposed</u> to <u>literary</u> or <u>learned</u>) . **perilous 1.** <u>involving</u> or <u>full</u> of <u>grave</u> <u>risk</u> or <u>peril</u>; <u>hazardous</u>; <u>dangerous</u>. **revelation 1.** the act of <u>revealing</u> or <u>disclosing</u>; <u>disclosure</u>. **bias 1.** an <u>oblique</u> or <u>diagonal</u> line of <u>direction</u>, especially <u>across</u> a <u>woven</u> <u>fabric</u>. **2.** a particular <u>tendency</u> or <u>inclination</u>, especially one that prevents <u>unprejudiced</u> <u>consideration</u> of a <u>question</u>; <u>prejudice</u>. **dearth 1.** an <u>inadequate</u> <u>supply</u>; <u>scarcity</u>; <u>lack</u>. **impeccable 1.** <u>faultless</u>; <u>flawless</u>; <u>irreproachable</u>.

abate—lessen
abbreviate—shorten
abbreviation—curtailment
abeyance—halt
abhorrent—detestable
abrasive—grating
abridge—shorten
abridgment—curtailment
abstinence—refraining from
abstract—nonrepresentational
absurd—farfetched
abundance—excess
accordance—agreement
acerbity—tartness
ache—yearn
acquiescent—agreeable
acquisitive—greedy
acquit—find not guilty
acrimonious—spiteful
activate—start
adage—bromide
addle—confuse
adept—capable, very able
adorned—decorated
affable—friendly
affected—influenced
affinity—connection with, liking for
aggrandize—magnify, enlarge
agitate—disturb the status quo
alleviate—relieve
allotment—share, portion
alloy—amalgamation
aloft—up high
aloof—distant, haughty
ambivalent—of two minds
amenable—willing, easy to persuade
amiable—friendly
amicable—friendly
amplify—make greater
amulet—charm
anarchy—chaos

ancestral—of ancestors
animated—lively, expressive
animosity—dislike
antecedence—act of going before
antecedent—predecessor
antipathy—dislike
antiquated—out of date
antique—very old
apathy—lack of caring
aphorism—adage
apparition—specter
aptitude—natural ability
arcane—mysterious
archaic—out of date
ardent—passionate
arouse—excite, cause interest
articulate—well spoken
askew—off center
assiduous—persevering
assume—presuppose
attentive—heedful
attenuate—soothe
attributed—ascribed
audible—able to be heard
auditory—aural
augur—bode
authentic—real
authenticate—determine provenance
avaricious—greedy
aver—swear, promise
avuncular—like an uncle
axiom—saying, bromide
balanced—sane, rational
banal—trite
banality—triteness
bar—ban
barbarous—cruel
barren—without life
base—low, common
beauteous—beautiful
bedlam—mayhem

beget—father, sire
beguile—enchant
beguiling—enchanting
bejeweled—adorned with jewels
belittle—make fun of
belittling—making fun of
bellicose—warlike, eager to fight
benign—harmless
berate—castigate
bestial—animallike
biased—slanted, prejudiced
biddable—amenable
blithe—carefree
bohemian—antiestablishment
bombardment—onslaught
bondage—oppression
boorish—coarse
breach—cross, encroach
brigandage—acting like a robber
bristle—take offense
broach—mention
bromide—adage
brusque—curt
cachinnation—loud laugh
cacophony—din
cadaverous—like a dead body
cadence—rhythm
cadge—beg
cajole—plead
callous—unfeeling
candid—frank, blunt
cantankerous—cranky
castigate—strongly reprimand
casualty—victim
cavity—hole
cede—give in, give up
censure—disapprove
certify—authenticate
cessation—stoppage
charismatic—fascinating
chastise—reprimand
chattering—talking a lot
chic—stylish
chide—berate
chromatic—colorful
chromium—shiny metallic element
chronograph—clock
chronological—in order by date
chronology—time line
churlish—rude

clamor—uproar
clamorous—noisy
clandestine—secret
clangor—ringing
clause—section
cliché—trite saying
coagulate—clot
coalesce—come together as one
coarse—rough, abrasive
coerce—force
cognizant—aware
coherent—sane, understandable
colossal—enormous
comatose—in a stupor
combative—ready to fight, belligerent
common—base, low
communicative—chatty
companionable—friendly
comparison—likening
compel—force
completion—finish
compliant—easily bid, amenable
complicate—make difficult
complicit—in on
component—part, piece
compromise—meet in the middle
compulsive—gripping
concede—acquiesce
concluded—finished
concord—agreement, peace
concur—agree
concurrent—simultaneous
condensation—dew
condense—compact
confection—sweet, candy
confine—enclose
congenial—amicable
conscientious—acting responsibly
conscript—draftee
consecrate—make holy
consecutive—in order, chronological
constituent—part; member
constrain—restrict movement
consume—eat, use up
consummate—conclude, finish
consumptive—having tuberculosis
contempt—disdain
contemptuous—disdainful
contentious—argumentative
contour—outline

contract—acquire
contraction—acquisition
contradictory—oppositional
contrary—as opposed to
conundrum—riddle, dilemma
convene—bring together
converge—come together
convivial—friendly
convoluted—complicated, difficult
convolution—intricacy
cordially—genially
corkscrew—twist and turn
corroborate—verify
cosmic—of the cosmos
cosmopolitan—urbane, sophisticated
counteract—act in opposition
counterfeit—fake
course—path
courteous—polite
covert—secretive
covetous—jealous, envious
cramp—contraction
crave—yearn for
credentials—qualifications
credible—believable
crescendo—peak, as in a musical piece
crux—linchpin
cultivate—work the land
curb—rein in
current—up to date
cursory—perfunctory; superficial
debase—humiliate; lower
debonair—charming
deceased—dead
deceptive—misleading
decimate—destroy
decorative—attractive
deduct—subtract
defame—slander
defection—abandonment
defective—flawed
defended—guarded
deferential—solicitous
defunct—extinct
degraded—ruined
delineation—demarcation
demised—dead
denigrate—speak ill of
depreciate—lower the value of
deregulate—free from legal restraint

derogatory—insulting
desirous—covetous
despise—hate, loathe
detractor—enemy; critic
detritus—debris, leftover
deviate—veer off course
deviating—changing course
devolution—transference
devolve—transfer
diabolic—devilish
diagonal—on an angle
diagram—drawing, layout
dictum—saying, adage
didactic—instructive
digest—take in; absorb
digress—veer off the subject
digression—conversational detour
dilatory—harmful
diligent—hard working
diminish—lessen
din—loud noise
discerning—intuitive, intelligent
discernment—insightful judgment
discharge—fire; let go
disclosing—revealing
disclosure—admission
discord—strife, disagreement
discordant—out of harmony, troubled
discredit—denigrate
disdain—contempt
disgrace—shame
dishearten—discourage
disintegrate—fall apart, deteriorate
disparage—denigrate
disposal—throwing away
disposed—inclined toward
disrespect—contempt
dissentient—a person who dissents
dissident—protester
dissimulation—act of feigning
distressing—upsetting
division—section
docile—passive
doctrine—policy
dogged—determined
dogmatic—opinionated, stubborn
dominant—on top
dominate—have influence over
dormant—at rest, not active
duplicity—underhandedness, deception

durable—long lasting
duration—extent, length
ebullient—full of joy, ecstatic
ecstatic—overjoyed
edify—instruct
effectiveness—producing good results
effervescent—bubbly
effrontery—impudence
effusive—overly outgoing
eject—dismiss, throw out
elegance—high style
elegant—fine, classy
element—piece, ingredient
eloquence—articulateness
emancipate—free
embellish—add to, embroider
embroider—embellish
emigrate—move to a new country
enchanting—charming, beguiling
endeavor—try, attempt
endows—subsidizes
engaging—attractive
engender—give rise to
engraved—stamped; etched
enhance—embellish
enigma—mystery
enjoin—order to do something
enmity—hatred
ennoble—make impressive
enormous—huge, colossal
enrage—anger
enterprise—business
entrap—snare
entrenched—dug in
enunciation—articulation
envious—jealous
ephemeral—short-lived
epigram—witty saying
epithet—nickname; handle
equivocate—be ambivalent
eradicate—wipe out, eliminate
err—make a mistake
erudite—articulate, learned
esoteric—confidential
essence—heart of the matter
ether—the sky
evacuate—send away
evict—forcibly remove
exaggerate—overstate the truth
exalt—sing praises

exasperate—annoy, frustrate
exceed—surpass
excel—do extremely well
exception—anomaly
excess—extra
excessive—too much
exclude—keep out, ostracize
excoriate—take to task
exhaustive—very comprehensive
exile—ostracize, evict
expedition—journey
explicate—explain
expurgate—remove offensive language
exquisite—beautiful, fine
extinct—no longer alive
extirpate—erase
extract—remove from
extraction—removal
extraordinary—unbelievable, wonderful
extravagant—lavish
extricate—remove
extroverted—gregarious
exuberant—celebrative
exultation—jubilation
facade—false front
facetious—jocular
facile—easy
facilitate—make happen, make easier
factionalist—person taking a side
fallacious—false
fallacy—false notion
fanatical—extremely zealous
fanaticism—zeal; fervor
fanfare—ado; big deal
fatal—deadly
fathom—understand
fawning—obsequious
felicitous—lucky in a good way
feral—wild and fierce
ferocious—vicious
festive—partylike, joyous
fetter—tie down
finery—best clothes
flattering—praising insincerely
fleece—rob, steal from
fluctuation—variability
foil—stop, hinder
foment—stir up
forcible—by power
foreword—preamble

foster—nurture
fraction—part, section
fractious—touchy
fragment—part, piece
fraud—fake
friction—personal conflict
froth—bubbles; soapsuds
frugality—thriftiness
fume—seethe
gape—stare
garnished—decorated
garrulous—outgoing
gaudy—tacky
gawk—stare
genial—easy going
ghoulish—macabre
gigantic—enormous
gilded—adorned
glamorous—showily attractive
gloomily—in a downbeat way
glut—excess
gluttonous—hoggish
goad—prod
grandiloquent—pompous
grandeur—magnificence
grandiose—conceited, pompous
gratify—greatly please
grave—serious
greedy—avaricious
gregarious—outgoing
grievous—deleterious
gruff—surly
hackneyed—trite
hamper—hinder
harass—bother
harbinger—omen
harmony—friendly cooperation
haughty—distant, cold
hazardous—dangerous
heterogeneous—diverse
hibernating—sleeping for the winter
hindrance—obstruction
hospitable—welcoming
hostile—unfriendly, of the enemy
humble—modest
hunger—yearn
hyperbolic—given to exaggeration
hyperbolize—aggrandize
hypothesize—theorize
idler—slacker

idles—waits, lingers
idyll—poem
ignite—start a fire, spark
ignoble—shameful
ignominious—disgraceful
illusion—fantasy
immeasurable—infinite
immoderate—not moderate
immune—safe from
immutable—not changeable
impassioned—full of passion
impede—hinder
impel—force
impenetrable—impervious
impertinence—impudence
imperturbable—stoic, unflappable
impetuous—impulsive
implicate—involve, as in a crime
imposing—dignified
improvident—irresponsible
impudence—impertinence
inability—lack of ability
inaction—lack of action
inadequate—not enough
inanimate—not alive, dead
inaudible—unable to be heard
inaugurate—commence
incapable—not able
incense—anger
incessant—unceasing
incident—event, occurrence
incisive—discerning
incite—ignite, instigate
inclement—stormy
inclination—leaning toward
incline—slope
inconsistency—lacking of agreement
inconspicuous—not obvious
incorrigible—not to be changed
indefensible—untenable
indefinitely—with no end
indelible—not erasable
indestructible—cannot be destroyed
indigenous—native
indoctrinate—teach; train
indomitable—not to be beaten.
inexplicable—unexplainable
inextinguishable—cannot be put out
inferior—lower in degree
infernal—devilish

infinite—having no end
inflamed—burning highly
inflate—fill with air
inflexible—rigid, unbendable
influence—sway
infringement—encroachment
infuriate—make angry
ingredient—component
inharmonious—out of sync
injurious—harmful
innate—inborn
innovation—new method or idea
inscribe—write on, engrave
inscription—ceremonial writing
insipid—trite, boring
instability—unsteadiness
instable—not steady
instigate—start
intense—hot; focused
intent—purpose
interval—gap; space
intimidate—cause to cower
intonation—way of speaking
intractable—not to be changed
intransigent—unyielding, stubborn
intrusion—encroachment
invention—innovation
inventory—merchandise supply
invigilate—to wait and watch
invisible—not able to be seen
invocation—prayer; chant
invoke—call upon
irascible—cranky, irritable
ire—anger
irrelevant—not pertinent
irreproachable—above or beyond fault
irreversible—permanent
isolate—separate, ostracize
jesting—joking
jocular—merry
jovial—in a good mood
jubilation—excitement, celebration
judicious—prudent, wise
justified—defensible; right
keen—enthusiastic
kindle—start, nurture
kinship—affinity
labyrinth—maze
lack—dearth
lackadaisical—slothful

lambaste—take to task
languid—slow, lazy
languish—pine away
languor—stillness
lapse—fall into disuse
lascivious—lecherous
lassitude—torpor
latent—hidden; already there
lateral—sideways
lavish—opulent
lethal—deadly
lethargic—slow moving
liable—responsible for
liberal—free; broadminded
liberate—set free, let go
linchpin—cornerstone
lingerer—loiterer
listless—lethargic
livid—very angry
lofty—high; superior
loiterer—lingerer
lucid—sane, clear
lurking—lying in wait
magnificent—gorgeous, incredible
magnify—make larger
majority—more than 50 percent
malcontent—person who is never happy
malevolent—evil
malign—speak ill of
malignant—harmful, cancerous
malleable—changeable
mandatory—imperative
marvel—wonder
marvelous—wonderful
mass—large amount, group
masterpiece—work of art
maternal—motherlike
matriarch—woman in charge of a family
matriarchy—group run by a woman
matricide—act of killing one's mother
maturation—growing up
maxim—adage
meander—wander
mediocre—average
melancholy—very sad, depressed
melodious—tuneful
melodramatic—over-the-top; overly dramatic
merge—come together
meticulous—very careful
misinterpret—misunderstand

monitor—watch carefully
monotonously—dully; tediously
monotony—tedium, boredom
moribund—declining; stagnant
morsel—small bit
mortuary—funeral home
motto—slogan
multifarious—assorted; diverse
multitude—many
mutation—transformation; change
naive—innocent
natal—pertaining to birth
nefarious—evil
nocturnal—of the night
nonadhesion—state of not belonging to
nonconformist—dissident
notorious—unfavorably well-known
novelty—something new; innovation
novice—beginner
noxious—poisonous
obdurate—very stubborn
obedient—amenable
obfuscate—deliberately confuse
objectionable—offensive; tasteless
objector—person who disagrees
obligate—morally blind
oblique—on an angle
obliterate—destroy
obscure—hide
obsequious—overly willing to help
observant—watchful
obsess—fixate
obsessive—fixating on
obsolete—no longer in use
obstinate—stubborn
obstreperous—argumentative
obtuse—dense, unable to understand
occult—related to magic or astrology
offend—insult, cause offense
ogle—look; stare at
ogreish—like an ogre
omens—portents
omissions—things left out
omit—leave out
omniscient—all knowing
opponent—competitor
opposed—against
optic—of the eye
optical—pertaining to the eye
oratory—eloquent speechifying

ornate—adorned
ornery—cantankerous
ostentatious—showy, overdone
outdated—antiquated
outgoing—gregarious
outmoded—outdated
overt—open, obvious
overture—opening gambit
painstaking—very careful
pallid—pale, unhealthy looking
pandemonium—mayhem
paragon—ideal example
paramount—chief, principal
parole—free from prison, with supervision
partisan—supporter; fan
passionate—avid
passive—amenable, do-nothing
peevish—irritable
penetration—infiltration
peninsula—land with water on three sides
penury—cheapness
perception—understanding
perceptive—having keen insight
perennial—coming every year
peril—danger
periphery—outline, outer edge
perishing—dieing
pernicious—harmful, dangerous
perpetual—ongoing
perplex—confuse
persuasion—ability to convince
pertinent—apropos
peruse—scan
perverse—willfully obstinate
petulant—pouty, whiney
phenomenon—wonder
philanthropic—generous to people
phlegmatic—dully matter of fact
pillage—loot; plunder
pitch—throw out
pivotal—important, paramount
platitude—trite saying
plebeian—of the common people
pledge—promise
pompous—pretentious
portent—omen
portion—part, piece
possessing—owning
pragmatic—practical
precipitate—give rise to

precursor—forerunner
predictable—expected
prediction—guess about the future
preemption—appropriation
prejudice—bias
prelude—overture
premeditate—determine in advance
premonition—intuitive feeling
prequel—earlier story line
prescient—prophetic
prescribe—order; recommend
presume—take for granted
presumptive—supposed
preventative—acting to prevent
primitive—first of the kind
proactive—anticipatory
proceeding—continuing
procession—parade; march
prod—goad, urge
prodigal—wastefully extravagant
prodigy—gifted child
profound—deep, philosophical
profusely—in large volume
progenitor—ancestor
prolix—wordy
prologue—introduction
prominence—conspicuousness
propagate—spread
prosper—flourish
protestant—dissident
prototype—model, first example built
protracted—drawn out
protrudent—thrusting out; bulging
protrusion—object sticking out
proverb—maxim
provocative—inciting
provocation—something that incites
provoke—cause, impel
proximity—nearness
proxy—representative
prudent—cautious
pubescence—puberty
pugnacious—confrontational
pulchritudinous—physically beautiful
pursuit—chase
quarrelsome—given to arguing
querulous—complaining
quiescent—peaceful
radiant—glowing
rapacious—predatory

rapturous—deliriously happy
rarity—odd thing
rasps—speaks with a rough voice
rational—sane, practical
raves—praises enthusiastically
ravishing—beautiful
recess—set back
recession—decline; turning back
recklessly—carelessly
reconnoiter—scout in advance
redeem—cash in
redundant—repetitive
refined—classy, elegant
refinement—good taste
refractory—obstinate
release—let go, set free
relevant—pertinent, apropos
renounce—give up
repetition—reiteration
reprieve—delay
reprimand—castigate
reproach—reprimand
repulsive—ugly, not alluring
reserved—staid in behavior
resigned—accepting
resolving—deciding
resplendent—adorned and bejeweled
restrain—hold back, hinder
restraint—curb; check
restrictor—something used to restrain
retain—keep
retaliate—repay or reply in kind
revealing—showing
revenge—retaliation, restitution
reverberation—sound; echo
revert—return to the way it was
revoke—take back
revolve—rotate
rhetorical—declamatory
rigid—stiff; fixed
rogue—scallawag
roundabout—circuitous
sagacious—wise
sanction—agree to, give the OK
sanguine—happy
sapient—wise
sartorial—of clothing
satanic—of the devil
savage—fierce; barbarous
scan—read quickly

scarcity—lack, dearth
schismatic—divisive
scorn—derision
scout—search for
scrupulous—principled
scrutinize—examine carefully
secluded—hidden, not in public view
sectarian—limited in one's interests
sedulous—persevering
seethe—burn with anger
sensationalize—play up for effect
separatist—person seceding from the church
sequel—later in time story line
sequestered—set apart, kept apart
serene—peaceful
servile—fawning
sheltered—protected from adverse conditions
shoddy—of poor quality
shrewd—savvy, wise
silhouette—outline
simultaneous—at the same time
sire—father
skew—slant, tilt
slander—malicious statements
slogan—motto
sluggish—lethargic
sociable—companionable
solitude—aloneness
somnolent—sleepy
soothed—eased
sophistry—simplistic reasoning
soporific—sleep-inducing
sordid—dirty, prurient
spare—backup
spectacle—public display
spectate—watch
speculate—question, wonder
spendthrift—prodigal
spiral—helix
sprightly—lively and energetic
spurious—false
squeal—shrill cry or sound
statuesque—tall like a statue
status—rank
steadfast—stable, responsible
stealth—sneakiness
stimulate—inspire; provoke
stinginess—miserliness
stricture—constraint
stridency—harshness

stringent—strict
stupor—daze
stymie—frustrate, hinder
subconscious—site of intuitive thinking
sublime—wonderful
subliminal—below the level of consciousness
submission—giving in
subscript—written underneath
subservient—obsequious
substance—matter
substandard—inferior
substantiate—prove
subterranean—underground
subtract—take away from
summary—synopsis
summation—closing statement
superannuate—become outdated
superficial—on the surface
superfluous—extra, not needed
superlative—the best
supplanting—replacing
surfeit—surplus, extra
surplus—surfeit
survey—scan, measure
swell—grow bigger
swerve—turn to avoid
synopsis—summary
tangled—mixed up
tantalize—tempt; entice
tedious—boring, endless
temerity—nerve; courage
temperamental—volatile
temperate—mild, as a climate
tempt—lure; entice
tenacious—stubborn, dogged
tendency—leaning toward
tenuous—uncertain
terminal—end
terminated—ended
terse—short, to the point
thoroughness—attention to detail
thrive—prosper
throb—pulsate
thwart—stop, hinder
tiara—crown
timid—hesitant, shy
toned—well-muscled
torment—torture
torpor—stupor
trace—outline, or small amount

tractable—obedient
tractate—essay
trailblazer—forerunner
transitory—fleeting
transmutation—transformation
transmute—change
treacherous—dangerous
trendsetter—leader
trite—hackneyed
triumphant—victorious
truce—peace agreement
truism—self-evident truth
truncated—shortened
tumult—uproar
tumultuous—noisy
turmoil—strife
tweak—tug; yank
twine—curl
ululation—mournful wail
umbra—shadow
unauthorized—not sanctioned
unbind—unfetter
uncompromising—steadfast; intransigent
unconventionalist—nonconformist
unfathomable—not understandable
unify—make into one
unleash—release
unmanifested—not shown
unnecessary—not needed
unprejudiced—not biased
unravel—come apart; untangled
unshackle—unleash, free
unsound—not safe, not secure
unyielding—uncompromising
urban—of the city
urbane—sophisticated
utopian—of a perfect world
utterance—saying
vacant—empty
vacate—leave
vaccine—immunizing agent
vacillate—be ambivalent
vacuous—empty
validate—certify
vanguard—leading wave
vanity—excessive pride
varnish—adorn
vast—wide, sweeping
vehement—emphatic
venerate—revere

veneration—adoration
ventral—pertaining to the belly
verbosity—wordiness
verify—prove
verse—poetry
vexing—perplexing
vibrating—oscillating
vicarious—experienced in place of another
vicious—cruel
vigorous—energetic
vilify—slander
vintage—from a previous age
violate—encroach, penetrate
virtuous—moral
viscera—innards; guts
vivacious—animated
vocation—employment
vociferation—clamor; ado
void—empty place
volatile—unstable
vouch—back; speak up for
vow—promise
vulgar—uncouth
wander—meander
weave—interlace
whimsical—fanciful
winsome—comely; attractive
witness—spectate; observe
woven—intertwined
yearn—want, desire
yen—hankering
yield—result
zealous—avid
zigzag—go back and forth

Index

Italic locators indicate answers to puzzles.

About the Authors

Jacqueline Byrne is a founding partner of Ivy Educational Services, a test prep and college application consulting firm with an excellent record of acceptances to elite colleges for its students. She provides private tutoring for the verbal SAT, the SAT II Writing exam, and the AP and SAT II Literature exams. After graduating from Yale with a B.A. in English, she worked for several financial institutions before starting a marketing company to provide creative development for clients including Chase Manhattan Bank, Chemical Bank, Neuberger & Berman, Yale University, and the University of Pennsylvania.

> The idea for this book came in a flash but grew out of years of frustration. Students with a weak vocabulary get a mediocre score on the verbal SAT. English teachers drill students every week in vocabulary; the students study the night before the quiz. When I tutor, one of the sentences I hear most frequently is, "I studied that word in school." They recognize the word, but they have no idea what it means. The current methods for teaching vocabulary are not working in schools, and they did not work for me. I want to change the structure of vocabulary study for the SAT. Word puzzles are excellent teaching tools, and they are fun for students—just as they are fun for adults. Adults choose to do puzzles, and so will high school students. As soon as I thought of combining puzzles with SAT vocabulary, I knew I had found the way to end my frustration. My students are grateful when I hand them puzzles for homework. I think SAT students across the country will feel the same way.
>
> *Jacqueline Byrne*

Michael Ashley's crossword puzzles have appeared in *The New York Times*, *The Washington Post*, *The Wall Street Journal*, and elsewhere. He has been a contributor to *GAMES Magazine* for 25 years. His ninth collection of puzzles, *Random House Crostics Volume 9*, will be published in November 2004. He is also a contributor to *Uncle John's Bathroom Reader Puzzle Book* series.

> Puzzles are about fun, of course. But there are other, more important processes at work when one is solving. Puzzles force you to focus your mind and organize your thoughts logically. They make you seek connections between words and meanings and then fill in the blank spaces of the words themselves—a spelling lesson at its most basic. Puzzles challenge you to be patient and to persevere; they ask you to exercise your mind and attune yourself to subtle allusions or oblique references. I have been part of the puzzle world for many years,

long enough to see it change from those old, hand-formed constructions full of abstruse, useless words—ancient Latvian coins, Madagascaran monkeys—to computer-enhanced works whose goal is to deliver puzzles containing only words one might use in a typical conversation. I think the modern puzzle with its wit and topical relevance is a perfect learning vehicle for the modern student.

Michael Ashley

Notes

Notes

Notes

Notes

Notes

Notes

Notes

Notes